Raw
and rare

Raw
and rare

Delicious raw, lightly cured and
seared dishes – from sashimi and
ceviche to carpaccio and tartare

Lindy Wildsmith

Photography by Kevin Summers

jacqui
small

For John

First published in 2017 by
Jacqui Small LLP
74–77 White Lion Street
London N1 9PF

Publisher: Jacqui Small
Senior Commissioning Editor: Fritha Saunders
Managing Editor: Emma Heyworth-Dunn
Designer: Maggie Town
Editor: Lucy Bannell
Production: Maeve Healy

ISBN: 978 1 910254 15 8

A catalogue record for this book is available
from the British Library.

2019 2018 2017

10 9 8 7 6 5 4 3 2 1

Printed in China

Quarto is the authority on a wide range
of topics. Quarto educates, entertains
and enriches the lives of our readers –
enthusiasts and lovers of hands-on living.
www.QuartoKnows.com

Contents

Introduction

IF YOU HAVEN'T YET TRIED RAW FISH AND MEAT, you may wonder what all the fuss is about — you may even find the idea worrying — but raw meat is not bloody, and raw fish is not fishy. Funny, that! Instead, if raw food is new to you, think of the flavour and texture of cooked fish or meat, then think of the taste and silky feel of their cold-smoked equivalents; raw is just a step away from the cold-smoked texture we are used to in smoked salmon. Now, think cooked vegetables versus raw vegetables — or cooked fruits as opposed to fresh fruits — and you may begin to imagine what a culinary treasure house awaits within these pages. Once you have tried raw food, you'll wonder what took you so long to come around to it. Raw food is light, refreshing, naturally sweet, reviving and satisfying. And, indeed, healthy.

However, this is not intended as a health book, but as an invitation to discover some of the world's most varied, taste bud-teasing and interesting culinary traditions, that have been enjoyed around the world for hundreds — even thousands — of years. Japan has sashimi, that reflects the seasons; South American cebiche (often spelled as ceviche) displays passion, colour and flavour; Italy has crudo; and France and Germany have tartare, all dishes that mirror the riches, style and sophistication of a broad culinary heritage. As people have shifted from continent to continent, from island to island, these raw food traditions have spread and evolved, creating new versions in adopted lands, using whatever ingredients were to hand.

Few people doubt the nutritional benefits of eating raw fruits and vegetables, but many are more sceptical about consuming raw fish and meat. However, these raw proteins have been eaten for millennia; in ancient times, in order to survive, and, in more recent times, for the pure pleasure of it. They are still enjoyed today by communities all over the world, wherever the tradition has lingered.

It is documented that, back in the first millennium, the people of Japan lived notably long lives, reaching eighty, ninety and even one hundred years of age, eating a diet of raw food and soup. They ate vegetables, fruit and nuts, and side dishes taken from a large range of raw fish and seafood, or wild game such as boar, deer, hare and duck. Fish kept the brain young, while meat aided growth and maintained health.

Whether you like to eat your fish, meat, vegetables and fruit raw and merely anointed or marinated; or seared, grilled (broiled) or blanched; perhaps lightly salted, smoked or pickled; there is something in *Raw and Rare* for everyone.

Sashimi is one hundred per cent raw fish, meat or poultry, filleted, sliced with extreme precision and served with dipping sauces and shredded daikon (mooli). It may be argued, however, that cebiche is not raw at all. The citric acid in the citrus fruits used in those preparations fundamentally change the proteins in the fish and meat to which they are added, in a process called denaturation. During this operation, the normally twisted and folded protein molecules are unravelled into less convoluted shapes. They lose their original nature, or become denatured.

Heat also denatures proteins; we call it cooking. High concentrations of salt denature proteins; we call this salting. Acetic acid in vinegar denatures proteins; we call that pickling. The acidity in wine denatures proteins; we call it marinating. Citrus juices denature proteins; we call this cebiche.

The meat and fish recipes in this book start with the raw experience, but they do not stop there. You may love fish, but don't fancy it raw, and there is no need to miss out; where possible, I have given instructions for cooking fish lightly before adding it to a dish. Seafood such as prawns (shrimp) and lobsters, squid and octopus are generally best lightly steamed or poached before eating, even if they are guaranteed straight from the sea (though I also give a fine recipe for raw langoustines here that is definitely worth trying). The dishes range from completely raw, through marinated, cured and smoked, to lightly cooked, so there are plenty of alternatives. But remember: anyone that enjoys fish and meat knows that – to get the best out of it – the flesh should be seared on the outside while retaining the moisture on the inside, which should remain rare. Overcook it at your peril!

Then there are salads and raw vegetable concoctions and dressings; a mighty store of pickles from Italy, Scandinavia, Japan, Germany and the UK to accompany fish or meat; and, to complete the picture, a colourful range of seasonal fruit platters with which to end your meal.

With this book, I am not asking you to change your diet, but to enhance it by enjoying a whole raft of thrilling new experiences, plus receiving the benefit – from time to time – of consuming the full raw power of nature, undiminished by cooking.

Fish and seafood

Getting started: fish and seafood

The chances are that — if you are interested in preparing and eating raw fish — you are already a fish lover and use a trusted fish shop or counter. If not, find one! Stay with it and don't be shy about using the fishmonger: ask their advice. Here are a few basics you should know, for the best results.

Choosing fish and seafood

Coastal dwellers from all points of the compass have long eaten, even lived on, raw fish. Fishermen all over the world have kept themselves going at sea by eating it. Today, this once elementary form of nutrition has been elevated to great culinary heights.

Whether making sashimi, cebiche, carpaccio or tartare, be flexible with your choice of fish once you are confronted with the display. You need it to be as fresh as possible, so choose from what is recommended rather than from a shopping list; use a reliable fishmonger and ask which fish they would suggest for eating raw. Without exception, the type of fish used in each recipe in this book can be swapped for another of the same type. You can mix and match fish and dressings in all the dishes. And remember: a good fishmonger smells of the sea, not of fish.

Buy fish and seafood in season; again, you'll need your fishmonger's advice on this, though there are useful online guides. There is pleasure in having to wait for something to come into season, then feasting on it while you can. Avoid imported fish where possible, unless it is of sashimi grade.

Once you have gained some experience in what to look for, the freshest fish will start to beckon to you. Whole fish such as mackerel, sea bream or sea bass should look as if they have just been pulled from the sea: open-mouthed, shiny-eyed and with firm plump flesh and bright-looking skin and gills. Fish fillets should be firm and plump with a silky radiance, showing no sign of leaching water.

RAW FISH WARNING

It is advisable to freeze all fatty and farmed fish for 48 hours before serving raw, to destroy any parasites. Although it is a shame to have to freeze oily fish such as salmon, it suffers very little or no deterioration when frozen for a short while. However, most white fish will lose its firm moist texture in the freezer, so make sure it is only frozen for the minimum amount of time.

HEALTH AND SAFETY

- Use a reputable fishmonger

- Buy fish and eat it on the same day, or at least start the preparation process, if it is lengthy

- Freeze fatty and farmed fish for 48 hours before preparation

- Wash your hands scrupulously before handling fish

- Wash utensils thoroughly before use

- Scrub chopping boards very well with salt, rinse and dry between uses

- Once fish has been prepared, store on the bottom shelf of the fridge and use within a few hours

Choose seafood carefully, looking for the same signs as you would search for in fresh fish: the flesh should be silky shiny, so if it looks dead, don't buy it. With a little effort, you should be able to imagine it still alive. Prawns (shrimp) should be plump and firm to the touch, dry, with no sign of leaching from the eggs. If you are going to eat them raw or lightly poached, always buy seafood with the shells on. Raw prawns (shrimp) are greyish or pale pinky beige and only turn red once cooked. Buy native prawns (shrimp) and langoustines if you can.

Scallops should not be white, but slightly beige in tone, wound in membrane with their corals still attached. If they are white, they have been left soaking and have become bleached. Hand-dived scallops are best, if you can get them. I remember, when I lived in Cornwall, that hand-dived scallops were all that was available. The fishmonger used to tip me the wink when a diver had been in. The scallops were still in their shells, straight from the sea. Yes, we had to wait for them... but boy, did we enjoy them when we could! I keep the shells, as they are perfect vessels for serving the scallops in.

Squid should look really shiny; not as white as snow, but rather streaked with grey, the remnants of its sepia. The tentacles should be still attached, and — if you are very lucky — the bag of sepia might be inside the body, too.

Molluscs such as clams and mussels should be firmly closed until cooked, at which point they will open (discard any that fail to do so). Their shells will feel rough and wild on the outside and silkily super-smooth within.

Sustainability

If you can buy wild fish, all the better, though make sure it is sustainable and remember that farmed fish is not always the answer to marine conservation, because it can create terrible pollution in the water.

It is difficult to give good guidance on sustainability, because the goal posts are changing all the time. What is off limits one year is back on the menu the next. Official guidance (and common sense) suggests the cook should choose as wide a variety of fish as possible and not stick with the same tried and tested type all the time. A good fishmonger will advise you on how to treat an unfamiliar fish, and be able to answer all your questions.

Eating raw fish

You may not have tried eating raw fish before but, let me tell you, once tried, you will be surprised at both the flavour and texture. Raw fish neither tastes nor smells fishy (if it does, don't eat it), but of the sea. It is firm to the bite, refreshing and sweet to the taste. The texture is something like smoked salmon.

When buying farmed salmon, freeze fillets for 48 hours to kill any parasites that may be present. Do not defrost the fish completely before slicing, but for just an hour or so, after which it will be truly firm and simpler to cut with precision. You may also like to freeze other fresh fish for 90 minutes before slicing, to make the slicing easier.

If you really don't fancy eating raw fish, try making my raw fish recipes but lightly poaching, grilling (broiling) or searing the fish first. It works well in most cases.

What to eat with it

The right accompaniments are also essential and are dealt with under each recipe. For my own taste I love eating bread and butter with raw fish, a habit I learned in Liguria, Italy, when I tried my first sea urchin. In Japan raw fish is enjoyed on its own, almost as pure protein, with a little garnish and a dab of dipping sauce. In South America, plantain chips, sweet potato, sweetcorn and popcorn often play a part in the mix on the plate, over and above the basic cebiche ingredients.

RAW FISH RULES

- Only buy fish from a reliable source

- Tell the seller it is to be eaten raw

- Allow 60-75g (2-2¾oz) for a starter (appetizer) portion, or 100-120g (3½-4oz) for a main course

- Be aware of hygiene at all times (see box, left)

- Don't wash fish; wipe with a damp cloth if necessary unless it is very bloody, in which case wash it in salt water

- Partially freeze fish for 90 minutes, to facilitate slicing

- Use a knife with a long thin blade; always keep it sharpened

- For D cuts, slice at right angles to the skin (see page 47)

- For long slices, cut at a wide angle, slicing towards the tail

- To slim down over-thick slices; lay them on a board and run a knife blade firmly and closely over the surface, stretching the slices as you do so (see page 43 for a photo)

- Make sure you use plenty of salt crystals and citrus juice either before or with the other ingredients. Raw fish needs more salt than you would expect; citrus juice kills bacteria

- Marinate for anything from seconds to 1 hour, depending on the recipe, or how rare you like your raw fish

- Serve with crusty white bread and butter, crackers, crisps (potato chips), plantain chips, savoury popcorn, even a cone of freshly cooked chips (french fries)... or by itself

Tuna loin and salmon 'tails'

It is wise to order these in advance. Your fishmonger will nearly always have them, but they are rarely on show. When you want to thinly slice tuna and salmon in a recipe, the tail pieces not only represent value for money, but you will need to buy less and there will be less waste, because if the girth of the fish is large you need to buy more to cut enough slices. The same goes for searing: if the girth is large, you would need to buy much more and cook it for longer, which would throw the recipes out completely.

Raw fish dishes

The beauty of experimenting with raw fish is that it opens up a wealth of healthy new ways to enjoy fresh fish. A good knife or two are essentials (see below), and so is a steel or stone to sharpen them on... but if you enjoy cooking, you will already have those.

Sashimi

A Japanese tradition in which raw fish are cut into slices that mirror the natural shape of each fish, arranged formally, then decorated with delicate leaves, vegetable shreds and flowers to reflect the season. Small amounts of soy-based sauces are offered, to dip into. There are also tiny heaps of grated ginger or wasabi to enhance the dish. At home a Japanese diner may enjoy a salad of sashimi, where raw fish is cut into cubes and mixed with vegetables. The whole experience is about the textures and flavours of different kinds of raw fish.

Cebiche

South American cebiche is traditionally cut into cubes, then marinated for anything from a few seconds to 10 minutes in lime or other citrus juices that denature the flesh. Chilli, herbs, vegetables and seeds are added to create a riot of flavours and textures. Sauces, dressings and accompaniments are poured over the fish, or served on the side and mixed in on the plate.

Crudo, carpaccio, tartare

Elegant Italian *crudi* (raw fish dishes) have long been popular up and down the peninsula. Crudo, meaning 'raw', is the generic word for all raw Italian foods (often referred to incorrectly as carpaccio). They owe their origins, just like sashimi and cebiche, to humble beginnings a very long time ago. Fishermen — having no means to cook or preserve freshly caught fish on deck — filleted fish to eat raw with a squeeze of lemon juice.

Carpaccio was invented as a raw meat dish (see page 80) in the mid-20th century, but the word is often used to describe raw fish dishes, especially those made from large meaty fish that give big slices. The fish – such as tuna, salmon or swordfish – is sliced thinly and served with a light covering of rocket (arugula) leaves, shavings of Parmesan, extra virgin olive oil and black pepper or even, as in the original meat version, with a light mayonnaise.

In France or Germany, 'tartare' generally refers to raw meat (see page 90) rather than fish dishes. However, formally arranged chopped raw fish dishes are often called tartares, simply because the fish is finely chopped, then moulded into a neat round, or shaped into quenelles with a couple of spoons, in the same way as a meat tartare.

Knives

Sashimi requires at least two knives, an all-round Japanese kitchen knife and a sashimi knife (see page 16). Cebiche, tartare and crudo need nothing more than good all-round kitchen knives. Remember, it doesn't matter how good your knife is, if you don't sharpen it at least once a day, it won't work.

If you are a fisherman and you are going to fillet your own fish, a filleting knife would be useful but — again — not essential. Ideally, buy your knife in person. Lift it, hold it, make sure it is comfortable for you to use. Don't buy a cheap set just because it is on offer. And, if you buy a knife over the internet, when it turns up, test it: balance it in your hand, see if it feels right.

Left: Preparing Avocado, radish, rocket (arugula), diced tuna and salmon roe salad (see page 22)
Opposite: Thinly cut slices of sea bass fillet

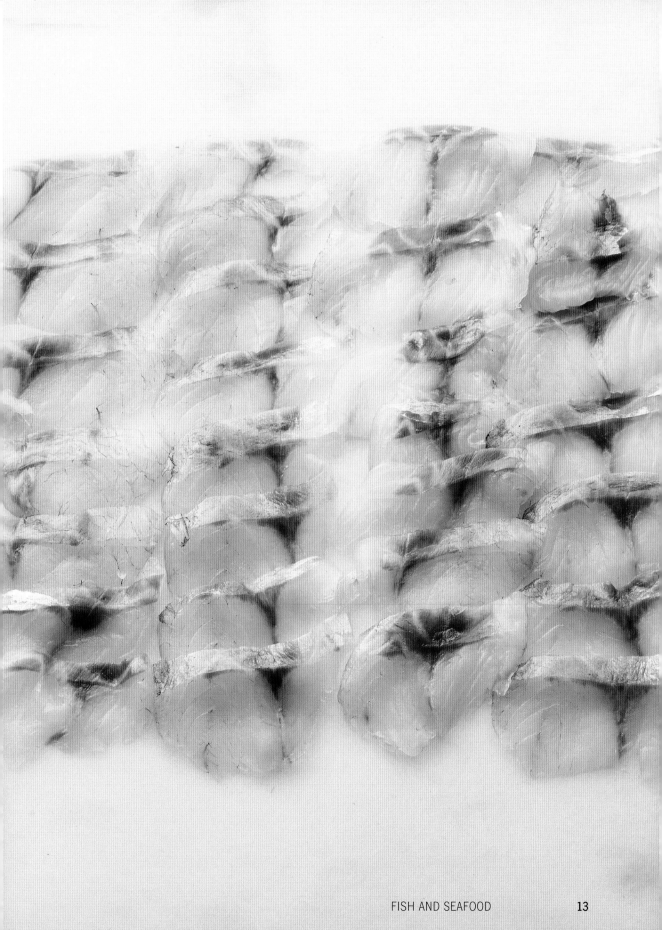

Filleting and skinning fish

Wipe the fish if necessary, then pat dry on a clean cloth. Gut the fish (if this hasn't already been done by the fishmonger), cutting down along the length of the underbelly, and scrape out the innards. Wipe the cavity with kitchen paper (paper towels) or cloth. Lay the fish on a chopping board and cut off the fillets according to the captions and photos (see right).

However good and experienced you are at filleting, you will need to trim the fillets of any bits of fins, bone and so on, and create a well-sculpted piece of fish ready for slicing. All this can be done a few hours in advance, but do not skin or slice the fish until required.

To trim the fish fillets, lay them skin side down. First, cut away the ribs that lined the visceral cavity, keeping the knife close to the bones to avoid excess wastage. Now you have to remove the pinbones that run lengthways down the centre of each fillet. This can be done in two ways. The first way is to use tweezers. Locate the pinbones by running your finger down the central line of each fillet, then pluck each out in turn. The second is to cut them away: cut a 'V' along and around the tiny bones that run down the centre of the fillets. Then, starting at the wide end of the fillet, pull away the V-shape of flesh containing the bones.

To skin a fish fillet, leave the fillets skin side down on the work surface. Run the tip of your knife between the fish flesh and its skin at one end of the fillet, creating a flap of skin that is large enough to grab with your other hand (a piece of kitchen paper / paper towel may help you to hold on to the slippery skin). Continue to cut away the skin, angling the knife towards the board away from you and pulling firmly with your free hand. You should find that the skin pulls away. For mackerel, the process is slightly different. Because their skins are so thin, simply nick a corner of it with your tweezers and pinch until you can firmly grab the semi-transparent membrane. Gently pull this off, leaving most of the beautiful, iridescent striped pattern of the skin on the flesh.

Below, from left: Skinning Dover sole fillet, mackerel fillet, salmon fillet

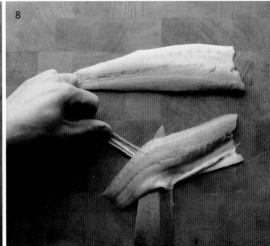

1   Cut the head off at an angle, close
    to the fins but passing the knife under
    the fins.

2   Slice down from the open cavity to the
    tail, keeping the blade flat to
    the cavity.

3   Turn the fish around and slice down
    from the tail end along the length of
    the fish's top side.

4   Turn the knife and cut away the fillet
    close to the backbone, towards the tail.

5   Turn the fish over and, working
    towards the wide end and keeping the
    blade close – but at a slight angle to –
    the backbone, release the fillet.

6   The fillets and fish skeleton.

7   Removing the pinbones with tweezers.

8   Skinning the fillet.

FISH AND SEAFOOD

Sashimi slicing and cutting techniques

The Japanese have eaten raw fish and meat since ancient times, a fact that has undoubtedly played an important part in maintaining the people's health. It was served as side dishes called *seisai*. To keep fish fresh away from the coast, it was salted or pickled in vinegar. The widespread popularity of sashimi only became possible with the advent of refrigeration.

Fish for sashimi can be salted. Lightly salt a board, put a piece of folded kitchen paper (paper towel) on top and a fillet on top of that. Repeat the layers – salt, paper, fish – piling them up, and finishing with a layer of paper, then of salt. Wrap in a clean cotton cloth and store in the fridge for at least an hour.

Generally speaking, thinner parts of fish fillets are cut into thinner slices at a wider angle; thicker parts at 45·. Cuts vary according to the texture, the flavour and colour, and the part of the fish.

The main sashimi pieces should be as big as the fish allows, say 3–4cm (1¼–1½in) wide (the width of the fish fillet) and 1cm (½in) thick. A firmer-fleshed fish is better sliced thinner and a softer-fleshed fish thicker. The important thing is that slices of a specific fish should all be the same thickness.

The sashimi knife, the *yanagi ba bocho*, has a unique blade and is forged in the same way as a Japanese sword from two different steels. It has a very long thin blade that cuts using little force. The blade is only angled from one side, being flat on the other, therefore is only sharpened on one side.

The cutting stroke of the *yanagi ba bocho* is like none other. The blade makes contact with the fish at the hilt and sweeps with a gentle curve, using the entire length of the blade, cutting through the fish and finally completing the cut in a single motion at the pointed end.

The blade is pulled through the flesh, rather than pushed. Practice makes perfect.

Note that, once cut, each slice is then inverted and overlaid to the left and slightly above the fillet.

Hira-zukuri (rectangular cut)

Fish with tough skins need to be skinned first (see page 14). In other cases, skin can be softened: have some iced salted water to hand. Put the fillet on a board, skin side up, cover with a double thickness of muslin (cheesecloth), put the board over the sink and pour boiling water over the cloth. Plunge the fish immediately into the iced water. Drain and pat dry.

Put a trimmed fillet on a board lengthways, skin side up, thick edge away from you, thin edge towards you.

Take the knife in your right hand and slant it slightly to the left. Secure the fish with your left hand. You will end up with your first rectangular slice, 1cm (½in) thick.

Each cut slice should end up on the tip of the blade; move it across out of the way towards the edge of the board, laying it inclined to the right hand side. Continue cutting and shifting the pieces to the right, one leaning on the other. When you have six slices, slide them on to the blade as they are and transfer, without disturbing them, neatly on to a chilled, garnished plate, leaning against the garnish.

Hiki-zukuri

A variation of hira-zukuri for softer, more delicately fleshed fish which might break up easily. Cut as for hira-zukuri, but put each slice directly on the serving plate as it is cut.

Uzu-zukuri (paper-thin cut)

Use this for good, firm fish such as sea bass and sea bream, sole and salmon, that will lend themselves well to the task.

Lay the prepared fish on the chopping board lengthways, skinned side down, thick side away from you, thin side facing you. Starting from the left hand side, and holding the knife blade in your right hand at an acute angle, almost horizontal to the board, cut slices across the grain of the fish. The slices should be no thicker than 2.5mm (⅛in). The firmer the fish, the thinner the slices. Each type of fish should be cut into identical slices. Lay the paper-thin slices on to a serving plate. Ideally, any pattern on the plate should be easily made out through the slices (see right).

Kaku-zukuri (cube cut)

Thicker, fattier round fish such as salmon, tuna and mackerel lend themselves well to this cut. Slice the fillets lengthways into 2cm- (¾in-) wide strips. Without separating the strips, turn the fish and cut at 2cm (¾in) intervals into cubes.

Ito-zukuri (thread cut)

Used for fish with very thin fillets. Cut across the fish in strips 2.5mm (⅛in) wide and 6cm (2½in) long. Serve in a little stack. Useful for creating a centre for a flower pattern.

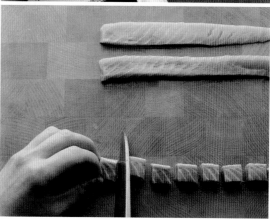

Opposite, from top: Uzu-zukuri cut sea bass and salmon; hira-zukuri cut tuna
Right, from top: Gossamer uzu-zukuri scallop and sole; overlaying gossamer-thin slices on a patterned plate; Kaku-zukuri cuts of salmon

Classic sashimi plate with shredded daikon, shiso leaves and ponzu

A classic sashimi plate features fish chosen according to season, and cut to show off texture, colour and skin marking. I have added salmon roe in an abalone shell to give a final touch of luxury. Do ring the changes according to what is available, and ask your fishmonger for the 'tails' of tuna loin or salmon (see page 11). Allow two or three slices of each fish per person.

Ponzu is a complex soy-based dipping sauce made in every home to serve with sashimi; each family has its special recipe.

Serves 8 small or 4 regular portions

For the sashimi

1 x 300–400g (10½–14oz) sea bass or sea bream

1 x 300g (10½oz) red mullet

1 x 300–400g (10½–14oz) mackerel

600g (1lb 5oz) tuna loin

600g (1lb 5oz) salmon fillet, frozen for 48 hours (see page 10–11), defrosted, patted dry

4 scallops

50g (1¾oz) salmon roe (ikura)

For the ponzu

2 tablespoons mirin

3 tablespoons sake

100ml (3½fl oz/scant ½ cup) tamari

4 tablespoons rice vinegar

4 tablespoons water

small square of kombu

5g (⅛oz) dried bonito flakes / shavings (katsuobushi)

4 tablespoons yuzu, or other citrus juice

To serve

250g (9oz) daikon (mooli)

crushed ice

thinly sliced radish (optional)

bonito or bottarga shavings (optional)

handful of shiso or perilla, or coloured kale, leaves, flowers and petals

finely grated root ginger

4 teaspoons ready-made wasabi, or a quail's egg-sized piece of fresh wasabi root, finely grated

Start by filleting the whole fish, wrap it as instructed and store in the fridge until required (see page 14). Freeze it and the tuna for 90 minutes before serving, to make it easier to slice.

To make the ponzu, heat the mirin and sake over a low heat for 3 minutes – to burn off some of the alcohol – with the tamari, vinegar and water, then add the kombu and bonito flakes. Leave to cool, add the yuzu juice, then strain into a screw-top jar and store in the fridge. It will keep for 1 month or more.

Shred the daikon either by hand or on the fine cutter of a food processor. Rinse in 2 changes of cold water, then leave immersed in ice-cold water for anything from 10 minutes–2 hours. Drain, dry on a clean cloth and store in a plastic box until required. This will keep for 24 hours in the fridge.

Just before serving, slice the sea bass (if using), red mullet, mackerel and tuna hira-zukuri, or rectangular style (see page 16) with the skin on (sometimes the skin is scored to allow greater absorption of ponzu). As you finish cutting each type of fish, arrange it on crushed ice. Cut the salmon, sea bream (if using) and scallops uzu-zukuri style (see page 17). Put the salmon roe in a small dish or shell.

Once everything is ready, arrange 2–3 slices of each fish on dishes filled with crushed ice. Let your imagination run riot, or keep it simple. Decorate the plates with the shredded daikon, radish slices, bonito or bottarga shavings (if using) and shiso leaves or flowers. Or line the fish up on a serving platter for everyone to share. Give each person a bowl, chopsticks, a dipping bowl of ponzu, grated ginger and wasabi. Any uneaten fish can be stir-fried the next day.

Hira-zukuri sashimi of sea bass with summer fruits

A great sashimi dish to serve when starting out, as it involves cutting just one type of fish in hira-zukuri style (see page 16). The combination of the fruit and raw fish also provides a good stepping-off point for the novice sashimi palate. The silky texture and acidic sweetness of ripe summer fruits make a perfect partner for any raw seafood and fish; use just one fruit, or a mixture. Slice the fruit thinly if you enjoy creating beautiful plates, and drizzle with dressing. Or chop the fruit, dress, mix and serve in tiny bowls alongside the fish or, as in the photo, on rose petals: all are authentic.

Serves 4 as a starter (appetizer)

For the sashimi

1 large sea bass or sea bream

petals, micro-herbs or leaves, to serve

For the yuzu dressing

1½ tablespoons yuzu, or other citrus juice

1 tablespoon rice vinegar

a few drops of tamari soy sauce

For the akincha ponzu

40ml (1¼fl oz/⅙ cup) tamari soy sauce

4 teaspoons Japanese soy sauce

4 teaspoons mirin

4 tablespoons sake

For the fruit (choose 1 or 2)

1 ripe-but-firm peach

1 ripe-but-firm nectarine

1 ripe kiwi fruit

4 large ripe strawberries

Start by filleting the fish, wrap it as instructed and store in the fridge until required (see page 14). Freeze for 90 minutes before serving (see page 11), to make it easier to slice.

Make the yuzu dressing and the akincha ponzu by putting their respective ingredients in 2 screw-top jars, then shake and store in the fridge until required. (Label the jars clearly.)

Score the peach and / or nectarine skin (if using) with the point of a sharp knife around the circumference one way, then repeat the other way, perpendicular to the first score mark. Put in a bowl and cover with freshly boiled water. Leave for 2 minutes, or until the skin lifts easily. Working quickly, take out of the water and peel, then plunge into a bowl of ice-cold water, or the fruit will cook. When cool, drain and pat dry. Peel the kiwi (if using) with a sharp knife. Cover all the fruit and chill until required. Chill the serving plates.

When ready to serve, cut the prepared peach and nectarine (if using) in half, take out the stone and cut the fruit into thin slices, or finely chop. Slice or finely chop the kiwi. Slice the strawberries thinly, or finely chop. If using sliced fruit, drizzle it with the yuzu dressing. If using chopped fruit, mix it with the dressing. Arrange the sliced fruit on chilled plates, or put the chopped fruit into individual bowls, or on petals.

Cut the fish fillets hira-zukuri, or rectangular style (see page 16), then place it on the plates in swathes.

Sprinkle with petals, micro-herbs or leaves and offer dipping bowls of the ponzu on the side.

Avocado, radish, rocket (arugula), diced tuna and salmon roe salad

A homely Japanese classic that can be served with shredded vegetables or sushi rice. The fish salad and rice would normally be served in separate serving bowls, allowing everyone to help themselves, mixing the two in their own bowls and dipping each mouthful in the dressing with chopsticks. I have served the sushi rice under the fish mix.

Serves 6

300g (10½oz/1½ cups) sushi rice (raw weight)

1 quantity Tosa vinegar ponzu (see page 24)

½ cucumber

1 large ripe persimmon

1 large avocado

juice of ½ lemon

6 spring onions (scallions)

100g (3½oz) cooked, shelled and deveined large prawns (shrimp)

200g (7oz) salmon fillet, frozen for 48 hours (see page 10), then defrosted and patted dry

200g (7oz) tuna loin

50g (1¾oz) salmon roe (ikura)

Prepare the sushi rice and ponzu in advance. (See pages 108 and 24.)

Shortly before serving, peel the cucumber, cut in half lengthways and, using a spoon, remove and discard the seeds. Put the cucumber halves cut sides down on a clean tea towel to dry.

Cut the persimmon and avocado into 1.5cm (¾in) cubes. Put into a bowl, add the lemon juice and mix lightly.

Cut the whites of the spring onions (scallions) into julienne slices and add these to the avocado bowl. Cut the green part of the spring onions (scallions) into very thin rings and set aside.

Cut the prawns (shrimp) into small pieces and cut the salmon and the tuna into 1.5cm (¾in) cubes kaku-zukuri, or cube style (see page 17) and add all these to the avocado. (You need 100g / 3½oz of cubes of each fish; use the trimmings for fish cakes or tartare, or freeze fresh tuna for later use; do not re-freeze pre-frozen raw fish.) Cut the cucumber into cubes and add to the mix.

Add 2 tablespoons of the ponzu to the sushi rice and mix lightly with 2 forks. Put in a serving bowl and top with the salad, letting everyone help themselves, or divide between individual bowls. Sprinkle with the green spring onion (scallion) rings.

Tumble the salmon roe over the salad and serve with the extra ponzu in dipping saucers on the side.

Oysters with shredded daikon and ponzu

Gone are the days when the oyster was an expensive luxury, oyster farms have put paid to that... yet finding oysters on a menu, or at the fishmonger, still gives me a thrill. A native is more flavoursome and is seasonal, available in autumn (fall) and winter; while the cultivated oyster is grown and therefore available year round. We are led by what the fishmonger has on offer... that said, I am a great believer in eating with the seasons.

Serves 2–4

12 oysters, rock or native, as available

For the tosa vinegar ponzu

40ml (1¼fl oz/⅙ cup) rice vinegar

40ml (1¼fl oz/⅙ cup) dark soy sauce

1 tablespoon tamari soy sauce

1 tablespoon mirin

6g (⅛oz) dried bonito flakes / shavings (katsuobushi)

10g (¼oz) square of kombu

80ml (2¾fl oz/⅓ cup) yuzu, or other citrus juice

To serve

250g (9oz) daikon (mooli)

crushed ice (optional)

4 heaped teaspoons finely grated root ginger

To make the ponzu, heat the vinegar, dark soy, tamari and mirin over a low heat for 3 minutes, then add the other ingredients. Leave to cool, then strain into a screw-top jar and store in the fridge (it will keep for 1 month or more).

Shred the daikon either by hand or on the fine cutter of a food processor. Rinse in 2 changes of cold water, then leave immersed in ice-cold water for anything from 10 minutes–2 hours. Drain, dry thoroughly on a clean cloth and store in a plastic box until required. This will keep for 24 hours or more in the fridge.

When ready to serve, open the oysters, but first rinse them in cold water and lightly scrub to remove any loose sand or fine debris. Wrap each oyster in a folded cloth with the hinge end poking out and the deep half of the shell facing down. Insert an oyster knife or other stout blade into the hinge and twist the knife, thus opening the shell. Cut the oyster free and return it to the deep half shell with its juices (strain the juices before returning them to the shell, if you prefer), discarding the flatter halves. (Should any debris have fallen into the oyster, rinse it before returning it to the shell.)

Serve the open oysters on ice, if you like, and give each person an individual dipping bowl of ponzu with daikon and ginger mixed in.

Langoustines with tomato jelly

This recipe was inspired by the tantalizing sashimi tomato jelly and langoustine dish created by Yoshinori Ishii that I enjoyed at Umu in London. If you have never eaten tomato jelly, it is a most extraordinary experience. The jelly is golden and crystal clear, bearing no physical resemblance to the tomato, but it is also very fragrant, reminiscent of the scent left on your hands after picking tomatoes. The taste gives you an umami rush that runs riot not only on the taste buds but also in the mind. Use fresh-from-the-sea langoustine, or other large local shrimp. If you only have previously frozen crustaceans, it is advisable to poach and cool them before using.

Serves 6

750g (1lb 10oz) ripe, juicy tomatoes (but not beef tomatoes)

3–4 sheets of gelatine

1 teaspoon salt crystals

6 ultra-fresh raw langoustines

1 tablespoon lemon juice

freshly ground white pepper

a few edible flowers, in season

Blitz the tomatoes in a food processor, then transfer to a jelly bag hung over a bowl. Leave until the tomatoes stop dripping. This will take a few hours; do not be tempted to squeeze the bag as that will make the juices cloudy. You should end up with a bowl of fragrant, pale golden liquid.

When the dripping ceases, measure the quantity of juice; you will need 1 sheet of gelatine for every 100ml (3½fl oz/scant ½ cup) of juice. Half-fill a bowl with cold water, add the gelatine sheets and leave to soak for 5 minutes until quite soft. Scoop out the softened gelatine with your hands and squeeze out the excess water.

Transfer the gelatine to a small saucepan and gently melt on a very low heat until liquid. Do not on any account boil it, as it will lose its setting powers. Add 100ml (3½fl oz/scant ½ cup) of the juice and stir, then take off the heat and add the remaining juice and the salt. Transfer to a shallow container, cover and put in the fridge to set. This will take a few hours.

When ready to serve, carefully remove the shells from the langoustines and remove the black tract. Put the langoustines in a small bowl, add the lemon juice and white pepper and gently turn.

Chop the jelly lightly and divide between shallow glass dishes. Top each with 1 langoustine and dress with edible flowers. Serve at once.

VARIATION: This is a sashimi-inspired recipe, but I know raw shellfish is not for everybody. The jelly also works wonderfully well with lightly poached langoustines (see page 63) and even with ready-cooked crayfish tossed in olive oil, lemon juice, pepper and dill.

Cebiche, crudo and tartare

Fish for South American cebiche is cut into cubes and marinated in citrus juices. It is then served with an array of colourful accompaniments that set the taste buds alight. Crudo and tartare, in the European tradition, are more subtle in flavour but no less seductive.

Cebiche

Cebiche is raw fish marinated briefly in citrus fruit juice. It is from South America, but there is no hard evidence to say which country invented it. Both Ecuador and Peru are in the running... although Polynesia has staked its claim, too. Peru's version of cebiche has a more formal reputation... which may or may not add to its claim to have originated this raw fish preparation.

Today, cebiche features on menus in every Central and South American country. Quay-side kiosks, beach-side shacks, stop-me-and-buy-one trikes, simple eateries and top restaurants all vie for accolades and customers. What must have started out as humble fishermen's food – and has long been little more than street food – has reached dizzying culinary heights, in top restaurants worldwide. Originally, freshly caught fish was eaten with the acidic tumbo fruit, a large banana-like passion fruit. Today the fish is more likely to be anointed with the citrus fruit juices and onions introduced to South America by the Spanish conquistadores. However, long before the Spanish arrived, the Incas preserved their fish with corn spirit and called it *siwichi*, which means 'fresh fish'.

Peruvian and Ecuadorian cebiche marinades are typified by lots of lime juice, chilli, onion and coriander (cilantro), with garnishes playing an important part. In Ecuador, popped corn and *cancha* (corn nuts) accompany the seafood, while in Peru sweet potato and lettuce are popular. In Nicaragua, plantain and banana chips often appear on a cebiche plate. In Mexico they serve *seviche* with tortillas.

The seafood in some versions is left for mere seconds to marinate; in others for an hour or more. The longer the marinade is left, the more opaque or 'cooked' the flesh becomes. Seafood such as clams, octopus, squid, prawns (shrimp), crab and lobster are often lightly poached or steamed first and added to the cebiche mix once any raw fish in the dish has marinated sufficiently.

CEBICHE GOLDEN RULES

- Onion slices and vegetable julienne should be plunged into ice-cold water to keep them crisp and – for the onion – to remove some of its pungency. Thoroughly drain and dry.

- Choose your favourite chilli, green or red. It is the white sinew that imparts most of the heat, not the seeds nor the flesh. I generally discard the seeds anyway, for aesthetic reasons.

- Coriander (cilantro) has a short shelf life, so make sure it is freshly bought or picked. Micro-coriander (micro-cilantro) looks good on the plate, tastes good and makes economic sense if you grow your own.

- Prep everything other than the citrus juice as near to serving time as you can, say 30 minutes or so.

- Cut the fish into bite-sized cubes; their precise dimensions will be governed by the size of the fish.

- It is essential that the citrus juice is freshly squeezed in your hands (not using a machine) at the moment of concocting the *leche de tigre*, dressing and serving the fish.

- Salt the fish. Salt crystals look beautiful and impart a special flavour. It is surprising how much salting raw fish can take, but don't forget to taste as you go.

- Add the *leche de tigre* and leave to marinate (see below). Pour off any excess into a glass and serve alongside the cebiche. Or serve the cebiche and the *leche de tigre* together in a tumbler or bowl decorated with cooked shellfish.

- Marinating times will vary according to the texture and the sizes of the different kinds of fish. A rule of thumb is simply to leave the marinade until the fish turns opaque, then taste it. The point is that the longer you leave the citrus juice on the fish, the more the fish denatures (or 'cooks'). The cebiche experience should be an explosion of freshly prepared ingredients in your mouth.

- Martin Alan Morales, London's unofficial Peruvian ambassador of food and culture, says to squeeze lime juice directly on the fish, marinate for seven seconds and serve. Oh, and never use anything mechanical to squeeze the limes. Fingers were made long before juice extractors.

- Solid fish, such as monkfish and hake, take longer to denature than sea bream or sea bass, salmon or tuna, halibut or sole. Mullet and sole take less time. Scallops don't take long at all; prawns (shrimp) longer. Squid varies, depending on size. This said, marinating time is also a personal choice. All may be lightly cooked before marinating, if you prefer (I feel octopus should always be cooked first).

Variations on cebiche

Nikkei is Japanese-South American cuisine. It has developed over a period of more than 100 years and helped shape what we today think of as cebiche. Peru has one of the largest Japanese communities outside of Japan. No surprise, then, that *Nikkei* should have given birth to its own cebiche style: *tiradito*, characterized by Japanese culinary purity in presentation and South American passion in colour and flavour.

In cebiche, the fish is chopped, but in *tiradito* it is sliced (as is sashimi), and *tiradito* does not generally contain onion or taste as fiery as its South American cousin. The *leche de tigre* remains common ground, but in *tiradito* it may contain mirin, soy sauce, sake, or many other typically Japanese storecupboard ingredients.

Ota ika, literally 'raw fish' in Samoan (or *poisson cru* in French Polynesia), is credited as being one of the possible regions of origin for cebiche. Indeed, a Pacific island seems its perfect birthplace, with its crystal-clear water and wealth of fish. The fish is marinated briefly in lime juice, then coconut milk and salad vegetables are added. Seafood such as mussels, sea urchin and eel are also used, and the name changes according to the type included.

Then there is *poke* (pronounced poh-key) from Hawaii, a simple concoction of chopped tuna, seaweed and sweet onion in a sesame and soy dressing that is sometimes served on warm vinegared sushi rice. This perhaps owes more to Japanese than to South American cuisine.

There are also Far Eastern raw dishes. *Hinava* from Malaysia is made with mango; *koi pla* from north eastern Thailand with freshwater fish, papaya and raw red ants; Korean *hwareo hoe* is thinly sliced, much like sashimi.

Crudo and tartare

Crudo is the Italian word for 'raw', used to describe any seafood or fish that is served raw. (The name 'carpaccio' derives from the famous Venetian raw meat dish invented in the 20th century, and is often used today to describe large slices of raw fish, such as swordfish, tuna or salmon.)

Tartare derives from the famous finely chopped meat dish, and is used to describe any chopped raw fish dish, usually in the French or German tradition.

I like Italian crudo served with a little olive oil, lemon juice and seasoning or — for special moments — crowned with the 'truffle of the sea': grated or sliced bottarga (cured, pressed mullet roe).

The sea urchin or *riccio* is king of crudi. The arrival of sea urchin season in late spring is much anticipated in high-flying restaurants and harbour-side eateries and booths in both Sicily and Sardinia. The seas around both islands are still clean enough for them to flourish and, there, the harvest is still limited to springtime. In the coastal waters around Puglia, they are harvested almost year round, and are already endangered. Like oysters, sea urchins come with their own traditions. I have enjoyed their lush, silky saltiness as an antipasto, served in the shell, cut open like a soft-boiled egg to be scooped out with a spoon or dipped into with freshly baked bread. Sea urchin stirred raw into al dente spaghetti is another glorious way to enjoy it. Be warned: you will need at least a dozen to make a single serving of pasta. Raw prawns (shrimp) are good too, served this way.

Shucked oysters are probably the most revered and popular form of crudo in the West. No high-end establishment in London, Paris or New York is ever without them. Oyster bars have sprung up the world over, even in airport terminals. No preparation is required once they have been opened. Serve in their shell, on ice, with lemon juice or Tabasco sauce and, possibly, a little finely chopped raw shallot in wine vinegar.

There's no limit to which fish or seafood you choose to eat raw, as long as it is in season, freshly landed and — for preference — wild. (Most farmed fish are fed man-made feed.) How you serve or cut crudo is up to you: smaller fish are sometimes left in fillets and immersed in marinade until opaque, which might take up to 30 minutes.

Classic cebiche with *leche de tigre* (tiger's milk)

It is said that the secret of making good *leche de tigre* is that it must be made by a Peruvian! That said, the more research I do, the more I find no two Peruvians can agree on how it should be made. Basic ingredients include lime juice, chilli, red onion, ginger, salt and coriander (cilantro). These ingredients, mixed with chopped or thinly sliced fish, create a milky substance, hence the word *leche* ('milk'). Add a splash of the local spirit, pisco, and *leche de tigre* morphs into panther's milk. With or without the spirit, it has a powerful reputation as an aphrodisiac and a hangover cure.

There are fancier cebiche marinade potions and concoctions, with added fish stock, orange juice, celery, garlic, squid ink… and even evaporated milk. These are often served as cocktails in elaborate glasses or tumblers with whole langoustines, squid and black scallops spilling over the top; a seafood cocktail as you have never seen it before. Hard-core enthusiasts dispense with the fish and just drink the *leche de tigre*.

Serves 4

For the cebiche

½ red onion

400g (14oz) super-fresh fish or seafood, or mix of choice, such as 300g (10½oz) sea bass or sea bream fillets, plus 100g (3½oz) large scallops

1–2 chillies

1 tablespoon chopped coriander (cilantro) leaves, plus more to serve (optional)

thumb nail-sized piece of root ginger, peeled and finely grated

2 teaspoons sea salt, or to taste

5 limes (traditionally these are Key limes)

To serve (optional)

4 whole cooked large prawns (shrimp) or langoustines

celery heart sticks with leaves

a few clams, lightly steamed to open (see page 56)

Peel the onion, finely slice, plunge into iced water and leave for 10 minutes.

Cut the fish fillets and scallops, or other seafood, into 1cm (½in) cubes and put them in a non-corrosive bowl.

Cut the chilli(es) in half, discard the seeds and the pith, chop finely and add to the bowl with the coriander (cilantro) and ginger. Drain the onion, pat it dry on kitchen paper (paper towels) and add this, too, to the bowl.

When ready to serve, add the salt and mix once. Then cut open the limes and squeeze the lime juice directly over the fish mix. Mix twice. Taste and adjust the seasoning as necessary.

Divide between 4 squat tumblers, or glass dishes, and garnish each with a large cooked prawn (shrimp), a celery heart stick and a small clam, or more coriander (cilantro) leaves, and serve.

Venus de cebiche

In Nicaragua, cebiche is as popular as it is in any South American country, whether eaten in the capital's restaurants, or bought from a trike on the quayside of San Juan del Sur on the Pacific coast. I was there for the *Fiera de productos pesqueres*, where I met Venus, dicing fish, cutting prawns (shrimp), chopping onions and squeezing limes. She was a vivacious and voluptuous young woman in a close-fitting dress, with glorious thick curls restrained by a hand-tied tiara of turquoise flowers. We tasted as she added chilli to the mix, a little at a time, until it was good. Job done, she filled stacks of paper cups for the waiting crowd.

Serves 4

200g (7oz) thick white fish, such as monkfish, cut into 1cm (½in) cubes

200g (7oz) large shell-on prawns (shrimp)

1 heaped teaspoon salt

1 small onion, finely chopped

1 celery stick, finely chopped

handful of coriander (cilantro) leaves, chopped

juice of 6 limes

½ green chilli, deseeded and finely chopped

Cut the white fish into bite-sized pieces.

Shell and devein the prawns (shrimp). (If you prefer to cook them first, drop into simmering salted water with a bay leaf for 60 seconds, or until just pink, then drop into iced water to cool. Dry on a clean towel.) Cut into small pieces.

Put the fish and prawns (shrimp) into a bowl, add the salt and stir once. Add the onion, celery and coriander (cilantro), mix, then add the lime juice and a little of the chilli. Taste, see how hot it is and – if you like – add some more. Serve at once.

Mixtos – dancing taste buds

An offshoot of cebiche, from Ecuador. *Mixtos* simply means 'mixed', and dishes of this kind would contain two or three types of seafood and a more complex garnish and dressing than that of a classic cebiche. This is my own take on mixtos; the 'dancing taste buds' name is because that is exactly the after-effect of this delicious and refreshing mix.

Serves 4 as a starter (appetizer) or light lunch

For the fish

2 small sea bream or sea bass, filleted and skinned, frozen for 90 minutes to make it easier to slice (see page 11)

4 large scallops or baby squid, cleaned and patted dry

2 teaspoons sea salt flakes

4 limes, plus lime wedges to serve

crushed ice, to serve

a few clams, lightly steamed to open (see page 56)

For the salsa

1 red onion

½ regular, or 1 small, cucumber

2 red (bell) peppers

small bunch of chives

2 red chillies

2 teaspoons pimentón dulce

4 tablespoons extra virgin olive oil

1 teaspoon sea salt flakes, or to taste

Start with the salsa. Peel the onion, cut it in half and finely slice, then plunge into iced water and leave for 10 minutes.

Cut the cucumber in half lengthways and, using a spoon, remove and discard the seeds. Put the cucumber halves cut sides down on a clean tea towel to dry.

Cut the (bell) peppers in half, discard the seeds, cut away the pith and cut the flesh into 5mm (¼in) cubes. Put in a small mixing bowl. Using scissors, snip the chives (you need about 4 tablespoons). Cut the chillies in half, discard the seeds and the pith and chop finely. Add the chives and chillies to the (bell) peppers.

Drain the onion and pat it dry on kitchen paper (paper towels). Dice the cucumber and onion into 5mm (¼in) cubes and add to the (bell) peppers with the pimentón, oil and the 1 teaspoon of salt. Taste and adjust the seasoning as necessary. Mix well.

Chop the part-frozen fish into 5mm (¼in) cubes and the scallops or baby squid into thin slices or rings. Put them in a non-corrosive bowl and, when ready to serve, add the 2 teaspoons of salt and mix once. Then cut open the limes and squeeze the lime juice over the fish. Mix twice.

Combine the fish and the salsa well and serve in glasses or glass dishes on ice, with lime wedges to squeeze over and clams, if you like.

Scallop and sea bream tartare with pimentón dulce and summer salsa

Pimentón dulce is a sweet and mild Spanish paprika that lends its colour and flavour perfectly to delicate fish tartares. I have added it to the salsa in this recipe but, when serving the tartare on its own, simply add a dusting of the ground spice before serving.

Serves 4

For the salsa

1 tablespoon extra virgin olive oil

pinch of salt

2 tablespoons cucumber, peeled, deseeded and finely chopped (see page 22)

2 tablespoons finely chopped red (bell) pepper

1 tablespoon finely sliced red onion

½ chilli, deseeded and finely chopped

1 tablespoon snipped chives

½ teaspoon pimentón dulce, plus more to serve

For the fish

200g (7oz) sea bream fillets, skinned

4 scallops (100g/3½oz)

sea salt flakes

3 unwaxed limes

Put all the ingredients for the salsa in a small bowl and mix together lightly.

Cut the sea bream and scallops into equal-sized cubes, put in a bowl, add salt, the finely grated zest of 1 lime and the juice of all 3 limes.

Divide between plates or dishes, top with the salsa and dust each serving with pimentón dulce.

Tiradito with samurai's milk

Tiradito was created in Peru, when Japanese and Peruvian cultures came together (see page 29). Samurai's milk is my Japanese-inspired take on the South American tiger's and panther's milks. Make this with any fish or seafood that takes your fancy, but make sure it is super-fresh.

Serves 8 small or 4 regular portions

For the tiradito

300g (10½oz) monkfish (tail end, see page 11), or other firm white fish, frozen for 90 minutes to make it easier to slice

1 teaspoon sea salt flakes

8 kumquats, or 2 small mandarins

100g (3½oz) cooked crab meat

juice of 1 mandarin

2 persimmons or 4 kiwi fruits

micro-herbs or leaves, or finely shredded seaweed, and micro-flowers or petals

For the samurai's milk

thumb nail-sized piece of root ginger, grated

50ml (1¾fl oz/scant ¼ cup) yuzu juice, or lime juice

50ml (1¾fl oz/scant ¼ cup) mandarin juice

50ml (1¾fl oz/scant ¼ cup) sake

2 teaspoons light soy sauce

1 teaspoon sansho pepper (optional)

Cut the fish into thin slices and arrange in a single layer in a shallow dish. Sprinkle evenly with the salt. In a small bowl, mix all the ingredients for the samurai's milk together. Halve the kumquats or mandarins, scrape out the contents and squeeze the juice into the samurai's milk. (Reserve the shells.) Pour the samurai's milk over the fish and leave for a minute, then drain, reserving the samurai's milk.

Season the crab meat and add the mandarin juice, then use this to fill the kumquat or mandarin halves.

Halve and slice the persimmons or kiwis and arrange in a line on plates. Lay a slice of fish on each slice of fruit, pour the samurai's milk over and add micro-herbs or scraps of seaweed. Top each serving with 4 filled kumquat halves, or 1 mandarin half, scattered with micro-flowers. Sprinkle with sansho, if using.

Sea bass with vodka, pink grapefruit and lumpfish caviar

Raw fish, whether sliced or chopped, and fresh fruit, whether sliced, chopped or puréed, make perfect bed-fellows. Try slicing strawberries and over-laying them on sliced monkfish with lemon juice and black pepper. Anoint sliced scallops with white nectarine purée and lime juice to create a silky smooth, sensuous starter (appetizer). Or do this!

Serves 8 small or 4 regular portions

1 large whole sea bass, about 500g (1lb 2oz), filleted, frozen for 90 minutes to make it easier to slice, then sliced paper-thin (see pages 11 and 17)

fine sea salt

1 tablespoon marmalade vodka, or other vodka

1 pink grapefruit

mint leaves

small pot of lumpfish caviar

Arrange this either over a sharing platter, or use individual plates.

Lay the thinly sliced sea bass on a plate in a single layer, season lightly with salt and splash with vodka.

Using a sharp knife, cut away the rind and pith from the grapefruit. Then cut into and take out each segment, working over a bowl to catch the juice. Trim off any remaining membrane from the segments.

Pour the grapefruit juice over the sea bass slices, then arrange the grapefruit segments on the fish with the mint leaves and lumpfish caviar. Serve at once.

RAW AND RARE

From left: Classic carpaccio of tuna; Carpaccio of salmon with whisky and raspberry vinegar (see pages 42 and 43).

Classic carpaccio of tuna

Carpaccio can be made with any large fish; all you need to do is slice it thinly and fill a plate. If you're feeling expansive, you can add thinly sliced cucumber, peach, nectarine, kiwi, berries or rocket (arugula). The best way to enjoy it, however, is the simplest: with just a little salt, oil and lemon, shavings of Parmesan cheese and — on very special days — with bottarga grated or shaved over: the salted, pressed and dried roe of either tuna or grey mullet.

Serves 8 small or 4 regular portions

300g (10½oz) tuna loin tail (see page 11), frozen for 90 minutes to make it easier to slice

juice of 2 lemons

4 tablespoons extra virgin olive oil

1–2 teaspoons sea salt flakes

bottarga or Parmesan shavings, to serve

Cut thin slices of tuna and arrange them on individual plates.

Put the lemon juice and olive oil into a screw-top jar. Seal and shake.

Sprinkle the salt flakes evenly over the tuna, add the dressing and top with bottarga or Parmesan shavings.

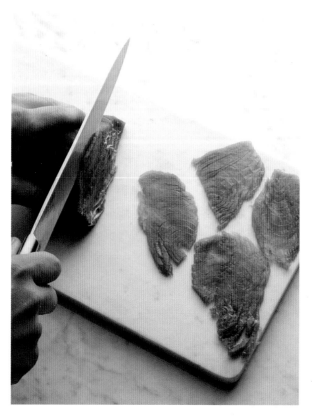

Left: Slicing tuna loin tail
Opposite: Slicing salmon; stretching the slices with a knife blade

Carpaccio of salmon with whisky and raspberry vinegar

Make this Scottish-inspired dish in summer and garnish with fresh raspberries; the note of sweetness in the raspberry vinegar lends itself wonderfully to a starter (appetizer). If you want to serve it as a main course, you can: simply omit the raspberries and the raspberry vinegar and add 3 teaspoons of lemon juice and a little Tabasco sauce. The dressing can be made in advance and stored in the fridge.

Serves 8 small or 4 regular portions

For the home-made mayonnaise

1 fresh free-range egg yolk

1 teaspoon Dijon mustard

sea salt flakes and freshly ground white pepper

75ml (2½fl oz/⅓ cup) sunflower oil

25ml (1fl oz/5 teaspoons) extra virgin olive oil

For the carpaccio

2 teaspoons whisky

2 teaspoons Worcestershire sauce

4 teaspoons raspberry vinegar, plus more to serve

2–4 tablespoons water

400g (14oz) salmon fillet, frozen for 48 hours (see page 10), then defrosted and patted dry

juice of 1 lemon

180–200g (6½–7oz/1½ cups) raspberries, torn in half

Put the egg yolk in a soup plate, add the mustard and salt and pepper to taste and, holding a fork parallel to the plate, whisk the mixture. Start adding the sunflower oil in a very thin trickle and, continuing to whisk in the same way, add all the sunflower oil. Then add the olive oil. This only takes a few minutes and is a simple and efficient way to make small quantities of mayonnaise. (Add 1 tablespoon lemon juice or white wine vinegar to taste when serving as a plain mayonnaise, rather than as part of a dressing, as here.)

Transfer the mayonnaise to a mixing bowl or jug and add the whisky, Worcestershire sauce, vinegar and water to dilute it to a pouring consistency. Chill until required.

When ready to serve, slice the salmon thinly and divide between individual plates. Sprinkle with sea salt flakes, then the lemon juice; pour over the dressing and scatter with torn raspberries.

Swordfish hinava with spring onion (scallion), ginger, chilli, mango and lime

The starting point for this recipe was a traditional Malaysian raw fish dish from Northern Borneo. In the original dish, the fish — either mackerel or tuna — is cut into strips and marinated in lime juice, then mixed with red onion, chilli, ginger, bitter gourd and the grated seed of a special mango, then served on a palm leaf.

Yellowish limes yield the most juice, while dark green limes make perfect julienned zest. If possible, buy two yellowish limes for juice and one with a dark green colour for this recipe.

Serves 8 small or 4 regular portions

quail's egg-sized piece of root ginger

1 green chilli

1 large, ripe mango (if you can't find ripe mango, use ripe peaches or nectarines instead)

4 spring onions (scallions)

2–3 large unwaxed limes (see recipe introduction), plus 1 more, cut into wedges, to serve

300g (10½oz) swordfish steak, cut 1cm (½in) thick

1 teaspoon sea salt flakes

Peel the ginger. Cut the chilli in half lengthways and discard the seeds and pith. Chop the ginger and chilli together very finely. Cut into the mango, sideways on either side of the stone, creating 3 pieces. Take the 2 outer pieces and, using a sharp knife, cut down to the skin in a 1cm- (½in-) square grid pattern (see photo, left). Turn the skin inside out and scrape out the cubes of mango. Eat the remaining mango around the stone! Discard the stone and the skin.

Cut the white part of the spring onions (scallions) into julienne strips and the green part into thin rings. Using a potato peeler, zest the dark green lime and cut the zest into julienne strips with a sharp knife. Juice all the 2–3 limes; you will need 100ml (3½fl oz/scant ½ cup) lime juice.

Cut the swordfish into thin strips, say 2cm x 5mm x 5mm (¾in x ¼in x ¼in). Put the fish in a bowl, add one-third of the finely chopped ginger and chilli mix, pour the lime juice over, stir and leave for 10 minutes, stirring once or twice more during this time. Drain off the excess lime juice and discard, then add the salt and stir once. The swordfish pieces should have become opaque. Add the mango, spring onions (scallions) and half the remaining chopped ginger and chilli mix.

Divide the swordfish salad between bowls and top with the remaining ginger and chilli mix. Top with the julienned strips of lime zest and a lime wedge. Serve at once.

VARIATION: Use seared swordfish steak instead of raw fish, if you prefer. Heat a ridged griddle pan over a high heat for 20 minutes, until white-hot, and griddle the swordfish lightly on both sides (say 1–2 minutes on each side). Leave to cool, cut into strips and proceed as for the main recipe.

Cured

This is really another way of saying 'preserved', and encompasses the practices of drying, salting and smoking fish and meat. All these methods have been used since time immemorial to preserve fish and meat in times of plenty for moments when food was scarce.

Large amounts of salt were employed, such as would be unpalatable to us today. We use fridges, vacuum packs and freezers to help us conserve our food and so there is no longer any need to employ such techniques, but we have been left with a craving for the intensity of flavours and textures created by these old ways.

Most countries have a salted, smoked or dried speciality that came into being long ago. Spain, Italy, France and Portugal all have their salt cod specialities, as do West Africa and the Caribbean, based on the rich Atlantic stocks of cod fished off the coasts of Norway and Newfoundland.

Britain has its kippers and smoked salmon, and Sweden its gravadlax and herring.

Salt cod and stock fish (dried cod) requires much soaking and rinsing to make it palatable before cooking, but today, with the help of refrigeration, we can create our own lightly salted specialities to make a genre somewhere between raw and smoked fish. This can be done either by salting and then drying the fish on a rack in the air, as for Malaga salted cod or Classic gravadlax (see pages 50 and 53), or by immersion in a 3.5% brine and then hanging up to dry, as is done in Japan. All these techniques create interesting and appetizing flavours and textures all of their own. Because the fish are only lightly salted to suit modern tastes, they should be used within a week or so. Incidentally, should you buy fresh fish that, for some reason, you are unable to eat straight away, bear in mind that salting is a better way to keep it than freezing.

In recent years, we have seen the arrival of the Himalayan salt block, a popular and quick means of enhancing raw fish, seafood or meat. It is 2–3cm (¾–1¼in) thick and used to salt-cure, but is pretty enough to serve the cured food on as well. Salt blocks come in all shapes and sizes — round, square, rectangular; small and large — and can be used at room temperature, chilled in the fridge, or frozen, as well as heated to high temperatures over a flame, on a grill (broiler), or even a barbecue. Or simply lay sliced seafood or meat on the salt block for a short time, turn it and leave it again, then eat the cured result. Salt blocks are a fun and rewarding item to have in the kitchen if you like to experiment, and they impart a unique salty and mineral flavour almost at the drop of a hat (see page 48 for a simple recipe). In short, they are great for the cook who likes to play in the kitchen, but by no means an essential.

For those that love the unique taste that salt-curing creates, but prefer cooked fish, the dramatic whole Sicilian fish in a salt crust (see page 74), where all the moisture is trapped inside, is well worth trying.

Left: Himalayan salt block with sea bass slices
Opposite: Slicing with a D-cut on a salmon fillet

Salt block-cured sea bream and basil pesto

First buy your salt block! If you haven't experienced salt block curing and cooking, it is a fun and fascinating genre to experiment with. Salt-cure fruit and vegetables, as well as fish and meat, in a fraction of the time it takes to salt using traditional methods. For this recipe, the salt block is cooled in the fridge or freezer, but it can also be used for cooking on a hob (stovetop) or barbecue as it withstands extremes of temperature. This pesto recipe makes more than you need, so use it up in dressings, for pasta, and with other fish dishes.

Serves 4–6 as a starter (appetizer)

For the fish

1 salt block

1 large whole sea bream (500g/1lb 2oz), filleted, frozen for 90 minutes to make it easier to slice, then sliced in D-cuts (see pages 11 and 47)

freshly ground black pepper

juice of ½ lemon

12 small basil leaves

For the pesto

½ bunch of basil

handful of pine nuts (about 20g/¾oz), toasted (see page 115, toasting as for peanuts), plus more to serve

1 walnut

1 garlic clove, peeled and halved

pinch of sea salt flakes

120ml (4fl oz/½ cup) extra virgin olive oil, plus more to seal the pesto

2 tablespoons finely grated Pecorino or Parmesan

Refrigerate the salt block overnight, or for at least 2 hours before it is required.

For the pesto, put the basil, pine nuts, walnut, garlic, salt and olive oil in a blender and blitz. Tip in the grated cheese and mix briefly. Pour into a screw-top jar. Don't waste what is left in the blender: add 1 tablespoon or so of boiling water and whizz again, then add this to the pesto jar, seal and shake well. For any that you don't use straight away, cover with a film of extra virgin olive oil, re-seal the jar and store in the fridge; it will keep for 1 month.

Lay the sliced sea bream on the salt block in a single layer, add a grinding of black pepper and a light squeeze of lemon juice and refrigerate for 10 minutes.

Take the block out of the fridge, turn the slices of sea bream over and spread them lightly but evenly with 6 teaspoons of the pesto. Return to the fridge for another 10 minutes.

Sprinkle with basil leaves and a few more pine nuts. Serve on the salt block with extra pesto for everyone to help themselves, or on individual plates.

Malaga salted cod with heat-blushed tomato and black olives

I first ate a combination of lightly salted cod and semi sun-dried tomatoes at a wonderful fish restaurant in the centre of Malaga, Spain. I complimented the chef, asked him how he made it and was politely told it was a house secret. Subsequently I discovered that this lightly cured cod is sold in delis there, just as smoked salmon is sold in Great Britain and gravadlax in Sweden... some house secret! I had cured cod in the past and it did not take me long to work the rest out.

Serves 8 small or 4 regular portions

1 tablespoon sea salt flakes	1kg (2¼lb) ripe tomatoes	12 or 24 small black olives (stone in)
¾ tablespoon granulated sugar	extra virgin olive oil	freshly ground black pepper
500g (1lb 2oz) cod loin, skin on	juice of 1 lemon	

Mix the salt and sugar in a small bowl and rub this all over the fish. Either lay the fish flat in a large plastic bag, or in a dish, and cover with cling film (plastic wrap). Leave in the fridge or a cool larder for 12 hours, turning from time to time.

After this time, wipe the fish down and lay on a baking rack in the kitchen for the air to circulate, to dry the cod. Leave it for 1 hour.

For the tomatoes, preheat the oven to fan 100°C/120°C/250°F/gas mark ½. Score the tomatoes, put in a bowl, cover with freshly boiled water and leave for a few minutes. Skin the tomatoes (the skins should just slip off) and quarter each. Deseed, mash lightly and arrange on a plate in the oven. Leave for 2–3 hours. Drizzle with extra virgin olive oil and leave to cool.

Slice the cured cod thinly, divide between serving plates and add the lemon juice. Arrange the tomatoes and black olives over the top and season with a little extra virgin olive oil and black pepper.

Serve with crusty bread.

RAW AND RARE

Classic gravadlax with dill sauce

It is essential to freeze salmon for 48 hours when you plan to serve it raw (see page 10), but for convenience you can cure the gravadlax ahead of time first and only then freeze it (again, for a minimum of 48 hours). This helps enormously when planning a party, or at festive times of year. You can then simply defrost it, make the dill sauce and serve.

Makes 1kg (2¼lb)

For the salmon

1kg (2¼lbs) salmon tail, scaled, off the bone, skin on (ask your fishmonger to do this), frozen for 48 hours (see page 10), or see recipe introduction

2 tablespoons sea salt flakes

2 teaspoons freshly ground black pepper

2 tablespoons golden caster (unrefined superfine) sugar, or honey

50g (1¾oz/2 cups) dill, chopped, plus more to serve

½ teaspoon ground cinnamon

For the dill sauce

5 tablespoons Dijon mustard

1½ tablespoons red wine vinegar

1 tablespoon caster (superfine) sugar

175ml (6fl oz/¾ cup) extra virgin olive oil

50g (1¾oz/2 cups) dill, finely chopped

Check the salmon carefully for bones by running your fingers up and down the flesh. Pull away and discard any pinbones with tweezers. Mix the salt, pepper, sugar, dill and cinnamon and rub into the flesh.

Lay the salmon, skin side down, inside a large, thick plastic bag. Seal the bag and leave to stand in the fridge for 24–48 hours as time allows; turning the bag from time to time. Alternatively, lay the salmon in a long shallow dish and cover with cling film (plastic wrap). Pour away the liquid that comes out from time to time.

Wipe away any excess cure with kitchen paper (paper towels) and sprinkle the fish lightly with fresh chopped dill. Lay on a rack in the fridge so the air can circulate around, and leave to dry for 2 hours. Mix together all the ingredients for the dill sauce.

Slice the gravadlax thinly and serve with the sauce.

Scandi salmon trio with dill: gravadlax, tartare and roe

This dish combines two popular Swedish ingredients: salmon roe and gravadlax. It becomes a trio of salmon by serving the gravadlax not only thinly sliced but also cut into cubes, tartare-style, and mixed into a salad of new potatoes: the classic accompaniment to gravadlax.

Serves 4

500g (1lb 2oz) piece of Classic gravadlax (see page 53)

200g (7oz) new or salad potatoes, cooked

1 avocado

1 tablespoon lemon juice

1 small bunch of radishes

3-4 tablespoons Dill sauce (see page 53)

1 small Cos (Romaine) lettuce

4 teaspoons salmon roe

dill, to serve

Slice half the gravadlax thinly, lay it on a plate, cover and refrigerate until required. Cut the remaining gravadlax into 1cm (½in) cubes and put it in a salad bowl.

Cut the potatoes and avocado into 1cm (½in) cubes and add to the salad bowl. Add the lemon juice and stir.

Cut the radishes into wedges and add to the bowl, then add the Dill sauce and toss lightly.

When ready to serve, divide the sliced gravadlax between plates. Make a nest on each of finely shredded Cos (Romaine) lettuce – or use a single leaf as a 'dish' – and fill with the salmon tartare salad. Top with 1 teaspoon of salmon roe – or put it on the side – and garnish with a plume of dill.

Serve with buttered rye bread.

Smoked, blanched, seared and grilled (broiled)

Hot-smoking is intense. Searing and grilling (broiling) are at high temperature, sealing succulence and moisture inside. All these are techniques that are perfect for oily fish. Blanching in water, stock or wine is a preferred method for serving all but 'straight from the sea' shellfish.

Smoke

The smoking of shellfish and fish fillets can be achieved at home, though hot-smoking is by far the easier option on a domestic scale.

Cold-smoking is done without direct heat. It produces fish (and meat) with a silky texture reminiscent of its raw state; smoked salmon is a popular example.

There are no recipes here that *have* to be cold-smoked, though I do give you an option to cold-smoke if you prefer. However, to cold-smoke, you need to own (or buy) a cold smoker – a major bit of kit – though if you are inventive you can make one out of an old filing cabinet, dustbin (garbage can) or fridge. As well as equipment, cold-smoking requires expertise and experience. It is a labour of love that can easily become quite addictive, though it is complicated and time-consuming and so – for the purposes of this book – I have assumed cold-smoking enthusiasts need little instruction here.

Hot-smoking, on the other hand, where heat and smoke are applied together, can be accomplished very simply at home, either in an old, well-lined steamer or wok, or even in a smoker bag. For a small investment, a table-top box smoker that produces professional results can be bought for the purpose. It is perfect for smaller items such as fish fillets, seafood and poultry breasts.

Blanch

Blanching is the perfect way to lightly cook prawns (shrimp) and squid. Drop prawns (shrimp) into simmering stock in their shells; the minute the shells turn pink, remove and drop into iced water to stop the cooking, then drain, dry and shell, keeping the heads and shells to make a shellfish stock.

Cut squid into diamond shapes and score their bodies finely on the surface that would have been inside, cutting the tentacles into short lengths. Drop into simmering water or stock, simmer for a minute, then drain and drop into iced water to cool quickly. Drain, pat dry and continue with the recipe you want to use.

Sear and grill (broil)

Searing fish – that is cooking it at high heat on the outside to seal the moisture on the inside – can be achieved in several ways: on a ridged griddle; under a grill (broiler); or in a heavy-based frying pan (skillet). I use all three methods, depending on which fish I am cooking.

A ridged griddle is perfect for searing meaty fish such as tuna and swordfish, but make sure the griddle is properly white-hot before putting on the fish. Set the griddle over a medium-high heat on a back ring of the hob (stovetop) for at least 20 minutes (that is not a misprint), then, when white-hot, add the fish. There is no need to oil the griddle. The fish will cook in minutes and release itself from the griddle surface when it is ready. If you have to tug at it to get it off, it's not ready yet!

Oily fish such as mackerel and sardines are really good grilled (broiled), as are fillets of sea bream, sea bass, mullet and similar types. Heat the grill (broiler) until it is red-hot before introducing the fish, lining the grill (broiler) pan with lightly oiled foil. Grill (broil) skin side up and, as soon as the skin crinkles and browns, take it away from the heat. Leave to rest for a minute or two before serving. Oysters also grill (broil) well if you don't want to eat them raw (see page 72).

To cook in a heavy-based frying pan (skillet) – the perfect way to sear scallops – heat the pan. Wipe the fish or seafood with kitchen paper (paper towels), then add olive oil or butter to the pan and sear the fish quickly on both sides.

... and finally

Though I don't have a recipe containing the technique in this section, steaming is a perfect way to cook shellfish such as mussels, clams, cockles and so on. Simply put them in a hot, heavy-based pan with the lid on. The shells will open and they will be ready in minutes.

Chilli and lime hot-smoked rainbow trout

If you want to cold-smoke this, double the quantities of fish and cure, to make the effort worthwhile. Smoking times are hard to predict and it is essential to check progress regularly. Hot-smoking times vary according to the amount of heat and smoke; cold-smoking according to the elements. Experiment with spices, herbs and citrus flavours, or with the type of wood.

Serves 4 as a light lunch or starter (appetizer)

20g (¾oz/5 teaspoons) coarse sea salt

20g (¾oz/5 teaspoons) granulated sugar

a few sprigs of coriander (cilantro), roughly chopped, plus more to smoke

500g (1lb 2oz) (about 4) rainbow trout fillets

finely grated zest of ½ unwaxed lime

½ chilli, deseeded and finely chopped, plus more to smoke

a little flavourless vegetable oil

handful (2 tablespoons) of cherry or elder chippings

Celeriac (celery root) salad (see page 126)

Combine the salt, sugar and coriander (cilantro). Sprinkle a wide, non-corrosive container with half the salt mixture. Lay the fish on top, skin side down, and sprinkle with the remaining salt mixture, taking care to moderate the amount of salt in proportion to the thickness of the fish. Top with the lime zest and the chilli, cover with cling film (plastic wrap), put a weight on top and leave in a cool place for 24 hours.

After this time, wipe the salt off, pat dry, put on an oiled rack and leave to air-dry for 1 hour. Add a few sprigs of coriander (cilantro) and some chopped chilli when ready to smoke.

To hot smoke: put the wood chippings in the base of a smoking box. I like to arrange them around the edge of the smoker as it creates a thicker smoke. Close the box and set it on a hot barbecue or hob (stovetop), according to the manufacturer's instructions, and wait for the smoke to start.

In the meantime, arrange the fish fillets on the wire rack. Once the smoke is billowing, slot in the fish tray and rack, close the box, reduce the heat, and leave to smoke for 5 minutes. Take a quick look, then close again and leave for another 5 minutes. Check again. The fish flesh will become opaque and smoky-looking when it is ready. Turn off the heat and remove the fish. Rest the fish for 10 minutes and eat hot or cold.

To cold-smoke: do so lightly and slowly. I cold-smoked 1kg (2¼lb) fillets, weighing 180g (6½oz) each, in my purpose-designed smoke box at 25°C (77°F) for 2½ hours (it was a cold, still evening), by which time they had lost the desired 10% amount of their starting weight and – more importantly – looked just right. However you chose to smoke the fillets, serve them as they are, or thinly sliced, with a squeeze of lime juice, Celeriac (celery root) salad and bread and butter.

RAW AND RARE

Japanese smoked skewered seafood with wafu dipping sauce

Hot-smoking is a great area for experimentation, following the basic principles here – marinating, drying and smoking – but playing with both fuel and ingredients. Use Mediterranean, Chinese and other flavours to marinate the seafood. Try other fuels such as rice or tea leaves, perhaps adding aromatic dried citrus and spices. Wafu is a fusion of Japanese dipping sauce and French dressing. You'll need 8 wooden skewers.

Serves 4

For the skewers

12 large prawns (shrimp), shelled and deveined

12 queen scallops, corals removed

4 baby squid with tentacles, cleaned

4 tablespoons dark brown sugar

1 teaspoon finely grated yuzu or unwaxed lemon zest, or 1 tablespoon sesame seeds

Pickled samphire (salicornia) and Shredded daikon and carrot salad, to serve (see pages 150 and 126)

For the marinade

1 tablespoon white miso

1 tablespoon mirin

1 tablespoon tamari soy sauce

1 tablespoon sake

For the wafu

4 tablespoons ponzu (see pages 18 or 24, however, if you have some already prepared, use that)

4 tablespoons extra virgin olive oil

1 garlic clove, crushed

Put all the ingredients for the marinade in a screw-top jar, seal and shake to combine.

Spread the prawns (shrimp), scallops and baby squid out in a shallow non-corrosive dish. Pour the marinade over evenly and leave for 30 minutes, then turn and leave for another 20 minutes. Pour off excess marinade. Thread 3 prawns (shrimp) and 3 scallops on to each of 4 skewers, starting with a prawn (shrimp) and pushing a scallop inside the curve of the prawn (shrimp) (see image). Then thread 1 squid body with its tentacles on each of the remaining 4 skewers. Lay on a rack and leave to air-dry for 1 hour.

Put the ponzu in a screw-top jar, add the olive oil and garlic, seal and shake to combine.

Line the base and lower sides of a wok with at least 3 layers of foil. Sprinkle the base with the dark brown sugar. Line the smoker lid with 1 layer of foil, taking the excess foil over the top of the lid. Put the lid on the pan, place over a high heat and wait for the sugar to ignite.

Lay the seafood skewers over the wok rack; this may have to be done in batches. Once the sugar starts to smoke, put the rack in place. Replace the lid, folding the overlapping foil in the pan up over the lid to contain the smoke. Smoke for 2–3 minutes, or until the seafood becomes a smoky amber colour. Make sure the prawns (shrimp) have turned opaque, as sometimes this can take longer, then transfer to a rack. Repeat with the other skewers until they are all ready. Check regularly, but be careful not to overcook.

Dust with yuzu zest or sesame seeds and serve as soon as possible, warm or at room temperature, with the wafu dipping sauce, Pickled samphire (salicornia) and Shredded daikon and carrot salad.

Scallops blanched in hot orange tiger's milk with sweetcorn and (bell) peppers

This is a warm cebiche, where the scallops are blanched at the table with hot citrus juice and vodka. Make sure you have all the ingredients prepared before squeezing the citrus juice and heating it. Serve in scallop shells, or shallow dishes.

Serves 4 as a starter (appetizer), or 2 as a main course

1 large sweetcorn cob

1 baby red (bell) pepper

1 baby orange (bell) pepper

1 baby yellow (bell) pepper

small bunch of coriander (cilantro)

2 small garlic cloves

1–2 red chillies, deseeded

8 large scallops (say 400g/14oz), plus 4 scallop shells, if possible

sea salt flakes and freshly ground black pepper

4 large oranges

2 limes

4 tablespoons vodka

a few chives, to serve

Strip the corn from the cob with a sharp knife, put in a blender and blitz to a fine grain. Tip into a bowl.

Chop the (bell) peppers very finely and add to the blitzed sweetcorn.

Keeping 4 small leaves back, chop the coriander (cilantro) with the garlic and chillies by hand, then add to the sweetcorn mix.

Clean the scallops, pulling off the corals, the foot and the outer membranes and blot on kitchen paper (paper towels). Cut 3 of the scallops into small cubes and add to the sweetcorn mix. Add 1 teaspoon of salt and a grinding of black pepper, then stir and taste.

Half-fill the scallop shells, or shallow serving dishes, with the corn and pepper mix.

Juice the oranges and limes into a small saucepan with a pouring lip. Add the vodka, bring to a gentle simmer, then switch off the heat.

Slice the remaining scallops thinly, say 4–5 slices each, and arrange around the edge of the scallop shells, or use small, shallow dishes instead. Sprinkle with sea salt flakes.

Put the shells or dishes on serving plates, propping shells on the edges to keep them level. Add a chive to each and the reserved coriander (cilantro) leaves.

Pour the hot orange marinade on to the scallops and keep topping up until the shells are almost full, or allow each person to pour the marinade over the scallops themselves at the table.

Blanched seafood melon

All kinds of ripe summer fruits — such as melon, peach, kiwi or nectarine — lend themselves well to raw or lightly cooked seafood mixes. Therefore, if you want to make this in summer, serve the mix in a melon shell. In autumn (fall) and winter, serve it in citrus or persimmon shells.

The secret of Japanese dressings is restraint; use just enough so that you know it is there and it enhances the flavour and texture of the fish and fruit without drowning it.

Serves 4

For the fish and fruit	sea salt flakes	For the dressing
200g (7oz) large squid, cleaned weight, bodies kept whole, with tentacles	1 melon or 4 large, firm, ripe persimmons	3 teaspoons light soy sauce
8 wild langoustines, or 4 North Atlantic prawns (shrimp), or crayfish		2 tablespoons yuzu juice, or 1 tablespoon lemon juice and 1 tablespoon lime juice

To prepare the squid, cut the bodies into 4cm- (1½in-) long diamond shapes and score diagonally on the inner sides into a very neat, fine criss-cross pattern. Cut the tentacles into equal, single-tentacle pieces.

Shell and devein the langoustines or North Atlantic prawns (shrimp). Don't waste the shells: use them to make a seafood stock.

Have ready 2 bowls of iced water, loosely covered with cling film (plastic wrap).

Bring a small pan of salted water to simmering point. Drop the shelled langoustines into the water and cook for 1–2 minutes until they just turn pink. Fish them out with a slotted spoon and turn on to a cling film- (plastic wrap-) covered bowl of iced water (this will cool them quickly without waterlogging). Drop the prepared squid pieces into the simmering water and cook for 1–2 minutes. Fish them out with a slotted spoon and turn on to the second cling film- (plastic wrap-) covered bowl of iced water. When the langoustines and squid pieces are cool, cut each langoustine into 3–4 equal pieces, put in a bowl with the squid, add the dressing ingredients and mix well.

When ready to serve, cut the melon in half (if using), reserving half for another occasion. Scrape out the seeds and cut the half-melon flesh into bite-sized bits. Or cut off the tops of the persimmons, if using (reserve these), scrape out the flesh and cut it into bite-sized pieces.

Add these fruit pieces to the dressed seafood, stir and spoon back into the melon or persimmon shells. Put the lids back on top of the persimmon shells (if using) and serve.

Blanched octopus in su-miso dressing

This classic Japanese dressing can be swapped with an olive oil-based dressing (see page 59) for a Mediterranean take, or why not try it with tiger's milk (see page 30) for a cebiche makeover. If you don't want — or are unable to source — a raw octopus, Japanese stores and some fishmongers generally sell whole, ready-cooked octopus tentacles, which, although rather expensive, simply need slicing.

Serves 4–6

For the octopus (if cooking from raw)

1 x 500–700g (1lb 2oz–1lb 9oz) octopus

300g (10½oz/1 cup) salt

1 tablespoon light soy sauce

For the su-miso dressing

2 tablespoons white miso

2 tablespoons rice vinegar

1½ tablespoons mirin

1 tablespoon Japanese soy sauce

½ teaspoon wasabi

If you are cooking a raw octopus, turn the octopus inside out, remove and discard the entrails, eyes and beak and put the rest in a large bowl. Add the salt and massage the octopus for 5 minutes. Rinse thoroughly in 2–3 changes of water and turn back the right way.

Bring a large pan of water to the boil and add the light soy sauce. Holding the octopus with tongs by its head, with its tentacles hanging down, carefully submerge the octopus 3 times in the simmering water, holding on to it all the time. Then drop the octopus in the water and cook for 5 minutes over a medium heat. Lift the octopus out of the water and hang it up carefully to dry with its tentacles hanging down, using an S-hook if you have one, from a tap over the sink, or from a cupboard handle over a bowl.

Combine the dressing ingredients in a screw-top jar, seal, shake and store until required.

When the octopus is cool, cut the tentacles off, then cut them on the diagonal into bite-sized pieces. Put in a bowl, add the su-miso dressing, cover and chill until ready to serve.

Pistachio-crusted tuna roll with watercress and grapefruit salad

Bronte is an agricultural town in Sicily, famous for its pistachio nuts and for giving the Bronte sisters their family name... but that is another story. Here you can enjoy pistachios in just about anything: pesto, liqueur, pasta... The nuts are sold in convenient packets already shelled and crushed in all their green glory; it is these you need for this recipe. If you can't buy them ready-crushed, put them in a plastic bag and crush evenly with a rolling pin: do not blast them to a powder, as texture is all-important here.

Serves 2

For the fish

300g (10½oz) long, thin piece of tuna loin tail (see page 11)

40g (1½oz/⅓ cup) pistachios, finely chopped or crushed

1 teaspoon sea salt flakes

1 heaped tablespoon finely chopped marjoram, oregano or parsley leaves

a little flavourless vegetable oil

For the salad

½ pink grapefruit

½ white grapefruit

1 tablespoon extra virgin olive oil

sea salt flakes and freshly ground black pepper

40g (1½oz/1 cup) watercress, or watercress and baby leaf salad

Roll and prepare the tuna in advance, at least 1 hour before cooking. Pat the tuna dry and roll into a sausage shape. Cut a piece of cling film (plastic wrap), large enough to roll the tuna in. Mix the pistachios and salt with the herbs and spread it out evenly in the middle of the cling film (plastic wrap), in a rectangle the width and circumference of the tuna.

Lay the tuna on the long edge of the pistachio and marjoram mix and roll it firmly to coat the fish all over; you may need to repeat this action once or twice until the tuna is fully covered. This done, roll the nut-and-herb-clad tuna in the cling film (plastic wrap), forming a 'sausage' and twisting the ends of the cling film (plastic wrap) to seal the roll. Store in the fridge, then – 1 hour before cooking – transfer to the freezer.

Preheat the grill (broiler) to its highest setting. Unwrap the roll, put it on a lightly oiled baking tray 5–7cm (2–2¾in) from the grill (broiler) bars and cook for 10 minutes until golden, turning now and then. Watch it closely (turn your back and it will burn). Now move the fish as far as possible from the grill (broiler) bars, switching from grill (broiler) to the highest oven setting for a further 10 minutes, for pink tuna. (For well-cooked tuna, cook for 20 minutes.) Rest for 10 minutes.

To make the salad, peel both grapefruit with a sharp knife, taking away pith and peel. Cut into segments between the membranes, working over a bowl to catch the juices, then drop the segments into the bowl.

Combine the oil and ½ tablespoon of the grapefruit juice in a screw-top jar. Season to taste and shake vigorously. When ready to serve, add the watercress or leaves and dressing to the bowl and toss. Cut the tuna into slices and serve with the salad, scattering over any of the pistachio crust that falls off.

VARIATION: Try cooking lamb, kid or rabbit fillets this way.

SALAD VARIATION: Try it with regular and blood oranges, when they are in season; serve with duck.

Fired bonito with shredded daikon and shiso
Katsuo no tataki

Kochi's seared skipjack tuna speciality is the centrepiece of the island's sashimi spread. Dark-red triangular fillets are lightly seared over wild flames. If you have a charcoal-fired barbecue and access to rice straw, you can try to emulate that traditional Shikoku method. Otherwise, I suggest using a ridged griddle. Bonito or skipjack tuna is hard to source in many countries; if this is true for you, use the tail end of a loin (see page 11).

You could also marinate a similar-sized piece of tuna in a mix of olive oil, tamari soy, garlic, rice wine and wasabi for an hour, searing it as below, then serving with rice and blanched samphire (salicornia) (see page 70).

Serves 4 as a starter (appetizer)

For the fish

½ fillet of bonito (skipjack tuna), cut lengthways along the lateral line, or the slim end of a tuna loin (see page 11), weighing 400–500g (14oz–1lb 2oz)

sea salt flakes

For the ponzu dressing

2cm (¾in) square of kombu

100ml (3½fl oz/scant ½ cup) yuzu juice, or half lemon juice and half lime juice

40ml (1½fl oz/⅙ cup) Japanese soy sauce

1 tablespoon tamari soy sauce

25ml (1fl oz/5 teaspoons) mirin

25ml (1fl oz/5 teaspoons) sake

5g (⅛oz) dried bonito flakes / shavings (katsuobushi), large flakes if possible

To serve

250g (9oz) daikon (mooli)

egg-sized lump of root ginger

12 shiso or perilla leaves

3–4 radishes, sliced

wasabi

If using tuna loin rather than bonito, trim off any bits that do not follow the contours of the main muscle. This will create a 'triangular' shape.

Make the dipping sauce a few hours ahead of time, or even the day before. Soak the kombu in the citrus juice for a few hours. Put the soy sauce, tamari, mirin and sake in a small pan with 1 tablespoon of water and simmer for a few minutes to burn off the alcohol. Switch off the heat, add the bonito flakes and leave to cool. Strain both the citrus juice and the cooled ponzu into a screw-top jar.

Shred the daikon either by hand or on the fine cutter of a food processor. Rinse in 2 changes of cold water, then leave immersed in ice-cold water for anything from 10 minutes–2 hours.

When ready to serve, pat the tuna dry on a clean cloth. Lightly salt each side and beat it gently but firmly with a rolling pin. Peel and grate the ginger finely. Heat a ridged griddle for 15 minutes over a high heat, or until white-hot. (Don't skimp on this time; if the griddle is not white-hot the tuna will not sear correctly.) Once the griddle is hot, sear the skipjack on each side; don't force it free from the griddle as this will tear the meat, it will free itself once it is ready. (Just give it a gentle push so it rolls over; if it doesn't budge, keep searing for a bit longer.) Transfer to a board and cut into 1cm- (½in-) thick slices.

Make a bed of daikon on a serving platter or individual plates, top with the tuna, decorate with shiso leaves and radish slices and serve with wasabi, ginger and dipping bowls of ponzu.

Seared mackerel with pickled gooseberries

This recipe follows the classic gooseberry-mackerel combination. Mackerel is a wonderful rich, moist, oily fish if cooked briefly at high temperature, either skin side down on a preheated griddle pan, or skin side up under a hot grill (broiler). The flesh should be just set. The robust flavour of mackerel and strident bitter-sweet of pickled gooseberries is a marriage made in heaven.

Serves 4 as a starter (appetizer), or 2 as a main course

2 sparkling fresh mackerel

fine sea salt

1 tablespoon extra virgin olive oil, plus more for the grill (broiler) pan

150g (5½oz) samphire (salicornia)

freshly ground black pepper

1 teaspoon white wine vinegar

1 jar of Pickled gooseberries with cardamom and star anise (see page 155)

Either fillet the mackerel yourself (see page 14) or ask your fishmonger to do so. Trim off any ragged bits. Cut out the row of bones along the lateral line by cutting a V-shape on either side of the bones. Cut or pull out the large bones that lined the visceral cavity. If serving the dish as a starter (appetizer), cut the fillets in half again lengthways. Wipe the fillets if necessary.

Sprinkle a little salt over a chopping board from 20cm (8in) above, to give a sparse covering. Lie the fish on the salted board, skin side down, then repeat the salt-sprinkling process and leave for 30 minutes.

Preheat the grill (broiler) until red-hot, say 15 minutes. Line the grill (broiler) pan with foil and brush lightly with olive oil.

Pick over the samphire (salicornia), discarding any tough bits, then rinse and drain. Plunge into simmering water (do not salt) and cook for 3 minutes or until tender. Drain. Transfer the samphire (salicornia) to a bowl, then mix in the 1 tablespoon of olive oil, a little black pepper and the vinegar.

Lay the mackerel skin side up on the grill (broiler) pan and cook under the hot grill (broiler) for 2–3 minutes or until the skin starts to bubble and turn golden.

Divide the samphire (salicornia) between plates and lay the mackerel fillets on top.

Spoon a few gooseberries on the side of the plates and drizzle 1 teaspoon of their pickling liquid over each mackerel fillet. Serve at once.

Franco's gratin of oysters with laverbread

This is one of Franco Taruschio's signature dishes, that he used to make for members of the foreign press when they visited our cookery school in Wales. Laverbread is a Welsh speciality seaweed, traditionally fried with bacon for breakfast. It is difficult to source outside of Wales, so I have adapted the recipe to use anchovy essence in its place.

Serves 4

20 native or rock oysters

100g (3½oz/scant ½ cup) unsalted butter, softened

1 shallot, finely chopped

1 tablespoon finely chopped parsley leaves

juice of ½ lemon

200g (7oz) laverbread, or 4 tablespoons anchovy essence

sea salt flakes and freshly ground white pepper

120g (4oz/2 cups) fresh fine white breadcrumbs

extra virgin olive oil

Preheat the grill (broiler) to its hottest setting.

First rinse the oysters in cold water and lightly scrub to remove any loose sand or fine debris. Wrap each oyster in a folded cloth with the hinge end poking out and the deep half of the shell facing down. Insert an oyster knife or other stout blade into the hinge and twist the knife, thus opening the shell. Cut the oyster free and return it to the deep half shell, discard the flatter half. Pour off, strain and reserve half the oyster juice. (Should any debris have fallen into the oyster, rinse it before returning it to the shell.)

Mix together the butter, shallot, parsley, lemon juice, most of the laverbread or the anchovy essence and the reserved oyster juice. Season with salt and pepper. Spread the mixture over the oysters and top each with a small spoonful of the remaining laverbread (if using). Sprinkle evenly with the breadcrumbs and paint lightly with oil.

Grill (broil) until golden and the juices bubble, checking regularly to ensure that the crumbs are not burning. Serve at once.

Sicilian sea bass or bream cooked in a salt crust
Spigola o orata al sale

This is a spectacular way of cooking fish: anyone who has been to Sicily will have enjoyed the show that comes when it is brought to the table and the salt crust is cracked open by expert waiters. Often the salt itself is moulded to mirror the shape of the fish, but we will be making a simple smooth crust here. The fish is not cured in salt, but buried between two layers of the stuff and baked. It may sound like a lot of hassle — and a lot of salt! — but once you are geared up, it delivers delicious moist fish every time; also, the salt can be used next time around. You can serve the fish with my simple home-made mayonnaise (see page 43) instead of, or as well as, the dressing.

Serves 2 as a main course, or 4 as a starter (appetizer)

For the fish		For the dressing
2 sea bass, 400g (14oz) each, or 1 large gilt head bream, 750g (1lb 10oz), cleaned	handful of fennel fronds	15g (½oz) fennel fronds
	1 bay leaf	3 tablespoons extra virgin olive oil
freshly ground black pepper	2 sprigs of thyme and rosemary (optional)	1 tablespoon lemon juice
1–2 garlic cloves	1.5kg (3lb 5oz/5 cups) fine sea salt	

Preheat the oven to fan 200°C/220°C/425°F/gas mark 7.

Dry the fish inside and out. Put a grinding of pepper, a clove of garlic and a handful of fennel fronds, the bay leaf and any other herb you are using inside the fish.

Put the salt in a large bowl and mix with 175ml (6fl oz/¾ cup) cold water to make a smooth paste. Line a non-corrosive baking dish with half the mixture, making a thick, even layer. Lay the fish on top, then cover with the remaining salt. Press the salt down firmly. Roast the fish in the oven for 15 minutes. Rest for 10 minutes, then break open the salt crust: you may need a hammer and chisel or similar arrangement, but take care not to stab the fish.

Meanwhile, make the dressing. Put the fennel fronds in a blender with the other ingredients and blast until smooth. Transfer to a small jug or bowl.

Serve the fish with the dressing and some home-made mayonnaise, if you like.

Meat, poultry and game

Getting started: meat, poultry and game

Raw meat has long been a favourite in Italy, so when Northern Italian Emma Morgano celebrated her 117th birthday, she revealed that her secret was eating a little raw minced (ground) meat every day... along with three eggs, two of them also raw. As good a reason as any for giving these delicious raw meat dishes a go.

The butcher's block

If you have a traditional butcher on your high street, or in your local farm shop, that is where you should shop for meat, as they will know where their meat comes from. However, if you want less mainstream meats such as venison, wild boar, kid, veal and so on, you may have to order it in advance, or shop around further.

RAW MEAT RULES

- Only buy meat from a reliable butcher who knows where the animals came from, and tell the butcher that the meat is to be eaten raw

- Allow 60–75g (2–2½oz) for a starter (appetizer) portion, or 100–120g (3½–4oz) for a main

- Be aware of hygiene at all times (see right)

- Don't wash meat; wipe it with a damp cloth if necessary

- Partially freeze meat for 90 minutes, to make slicing easier

- Use a large kitchen knife for chopping and slicing; sharpen it before use (though if you have a meat slicer you really can achieve paper-thin slices)

- To slim down over-thick slices, lay them on a board and run a knife blade firmly and closely over the surface, stretching the slices as you do so

- Make sure you use plenty of salt for the best flavour; raw protein requires more salt than you would expect. Salt also inhibits the growth of bacteria

- Citrus juice kills bacteria but it also denatures or 'cooks' the protein and changes the taste and texture, so do not leave meat in citrus juice for too long if you want pink meat

- Marinate meat for anything from seconds to an hour, depending on how rare you like it

- Serve raw meat with pickles, sourdough, crusty white or black rye bread and butter, a cone of freshly cooked chips, or with a celeriac (celery root) or other salad (see pages 122–143)

Tell your expert butcher what you want and, especially, how you are going to prepare it. Fillets and loins are the best cuts to go for to eat raw, as they offer the most tender meat. Rump (top round) and sirloin (short loin) steaks are good, too. Fillet (tenderloin) tails are excellent; your butcher will usually have these, but not often on show, and they are excellent value for money, especially when you want to slice the meat thinly in a recipe. Skirt is good for marinated dishes. All of my recipes recommend the best cuts and types of meats to use.

Choosing raw meat

Meats such as pork, rabbit, veal, lamb and kid should look fresh and pink. (Pork is quite safe to eat raw nowadays, but I find raw pork tastes of the farmyard and prefer to eat it cooked.) Beef, venison and wild boar should be dark red.

The cuts of meat should be the same colour all the way through, showing no signs of browning around the outside, which might well indicate it is not as fresh as you would like.

I do not recommend eating chicken or other poultry raw, or any game birds that have been well hung. However, farmed duck breast makes a great smoked or seared dish (see pages 112 and 115).

Preparing raw meat

When it comes to preparing it at home, there is no more danger in eating fresh raw meat than cooked meat. Some of us do, some don't; some will, some won't. The most important rule to observe when serving and eating raw meat, as already mentioned, is to always buy it from a reliable local source that knows the provenance of the animals they sell. I don't (and wouldn't) buy meat in a supermarket to eat raw, for this reason.

After you buy your meat, refrigerate it. Always slice, chop or mince (grind) the meat yourself, using scrupulously clean equipment, under hygienic conditions (see box, right). Contamination generally occurs during unseen, unhygienic processing, not under domestic kitchen conditions, as long as you follow the rules.

HEALTH AND SAFETY

- Use a reputable butcher

- Buy the meat and eat it on the same day

- Chop or slice it yourself

- Wash your hands scrupulously before handling meat

- Wash utensils thoroughly before use

- Scrub chopping boards very well with salt, rinse and dry between uses

- Once the meat has been prepared, store carefully on the bottom shelf of the fridge and use within a few hours

Raw meat dishes: carpaccio and *la carne cruda*

The Italians are masters at raw meat, the literal meaning of *carne cruda*. The original dish of rose veal, sliced paper-thin, came from Alba in Piedmont, Italy. Carpaccio was created much later, as a dish of thinly sliced beef, but the term has gone viral and is now used globally to describe anything, raw or otherwise, that is thinly sliced.

Giuseppe Cipriani, founder of Harry's Bar in Venice, Italy, and his son Arrigo, first developed a dish of very thinly carved raw fillet (tenderloin) steak dressed with a light mayonnaise sauce in the mid-20th century, to please one of their rich clients. At the time there was in the city a show of the work of the 16th-century Venetian School painter, Vittorio Carpaccio. Carpaccio's paintings are known for their bright (raw beef) red and, when Cipriani saw a poster advertising the exhibition, he coined the name for his recipe. The dish caught on and the rest is history… or is it?

Because there was a thinly sliced, raw meat dish known as *La cruda all'albese* or *Insalata di carne cruda* (literally 'salad of raw meat') in Piedmont in Northern Italy long before then. It consists of thinly sliced fillet (tenderloin) of beef or veal with white truffle and extra virgin olive oil. Beyond the truffle season, the beef is sometimes topped with thinly sliced porcini or ovoli mushrooms, or simply with rocket (arugula) leaves and Parmesan shavings. This original dish, today, has come to be incorrectly but almost universally known as carpaccio. The Italian regions are proud of their heritage and are outstandingly partisan, so it's important to make this distinction clear.

There are myriad variations on the theme: olive oil, lemon juice, salt and freshly ground black pepper are pretty much constants, not to forget the garnish of rocket (arugula) leaves, or sliced artichokes, mushrooms or other vegetables. Other citrus fruit juices can be used instead of lemon; fresh herbs, pestos made with herbs and nuts; toasted almonds, pistachios and pine nuts; balsamic vinegar, chilli and tomato all take their bows. And the cheese need not start and finish with Parmesan; Gorgonzola, pecorino and even Stilton works.

However, call it carpaccio or *carne cruda*, the meat is sliced and laid out on plates, the garnish added, the dressing poured over and the dish served straight away, to stunning effect.

I use wagyu in one of the recipes in this section. Wagyu means 'Japanese beef'. Its chief characteristic is the heavy marbling of fat, resembling the veins of a cabbage leaf (see photo, left). It is butter-tender, exquisitely flavoured, juicy… and hugely expensive. It is a real and rare treat and is now available overseas.

Australian 'wagyu' has been around for some time, and beef breeders across the world are giving it a try. However, my opinion is that made in Japan is the only way to go if you want wagyu! The secret is not just in the breed, but in how it is bred.

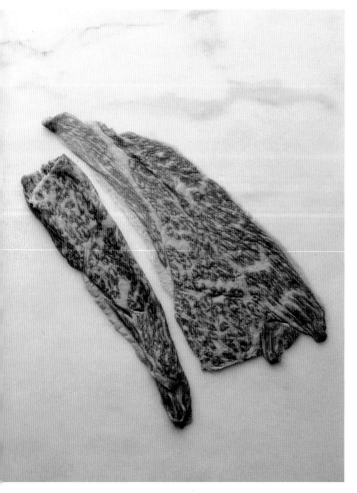

Left: Slices of wagyu (Japanese beef)
Opposite: Slicing raw beef for carpaccio

Harry's Bar carpaccio

We can't be certain where the original carpaccio recipe came from. What we do know is that it was a plate of thinly sliced fillet (tenderloin) of beef served with a thin mayonnaise dressing. The mayonnaise was diluted – possibly with water or milk – spiked with whisky or brandy and flavoured with Worcestershire sauce and / or Tabasco. Some say an inflection of ketchup adds a pleasing note of sweetness. However, in my mind – tainted as it is by lurid, pink thousand island dressings – I cannot even contemplate the idea. Some versions include lemon juice, but this would surely 'cook' the meat and spoil the dish. So this is my interpretation. The dressing can be made in advance and stored in the fridge.

Serves 8 small or 4 regular portions

400g (14oz) chilled fillet (tenderloin) steak

1 x quantity Home-made mayonnaise (see page 43)

2 teaspoons brandy

2 teaspoons Worcestershire sauce

a few drops of Tabasco sauce

4 tablespoons water

sea salt flakes and freshly ground black pepper

Freeze the meat for 90 minutes before slicing, as this will help with the cutting process. It is always best to cut the meat and serve it straight away, but you may prefer to slice it up to 2 hours before serving (pile the meat on a plate, cover completely with cling film / plastic wrap and refrigerate until required). It will still be good.

Put the mayonnaise in a mixing bowl or jug and add the brandy, Worcestershire and Tabasco sauces and the water, to dilute it to a pouring consistency. Cover and put in the fridge until required.

Divide the steak between plates and add the dressing. Serve straight away, offering salt flakes and pepper at the table.

VARIATIONS: Add ½ teaspoon grated horseradish or wasabi to the dressing for extra fire; or try sprinkling the carpaccio with chopped capers, or anchovies and grated Parmesan cheese, for more depth of flavour.

La carne cruda all'albese

Long before the much-celebrated carpaccio was dreamed up in Venice, Italy, *la carne cruda all'albese* was a well-known antipasto speciality from Alba, popular throughout the whole of the Italian Piedmont region. It consists of raw, thinly sliced or finely chopped veal, in a lemon juice and extra virgin olive oil dressing, fragranced with garlic. In autumn, the lemon juice is omitted and shavings of Alba's famous white truffle are added. Porcini or ovoli mushrooms are also popular additions. These raw meat antipasti have become universally but incorrectly known as *carpacci*.

Serves 4

4 tablespoons extra virgin olive oil

juice of 1 lemon

1 garlic clove, squashed with the side of a knife and peeled

pinch of fine sea salt and a grinding of freshly ground black pepper

400g (14oz) chilled fillet of rose veal, frozen for 90 minutes before slicing to make it easier to slice, thinly sliced (see page 78)

Put the oil in a screw-top jar with the lemon juice, garlic, salt and pepper. Seal with the lid and shake well.

When ready to serve, lay the meat out on a large plate and splash the dressing over it all. It is traditional to do this 15 minutes before serving, to 'cook' or denature the meat in the lemon juice, but if you prefer your meat *au naturel*, add the dressing just before serving. Serve straight away.

VARIATIONS: Omit the lemon juice and add shaved white truffle. If you want to add porcini or ovoli mushrooms, keep one-third of the dressing back to marinate the thinly sliced mushrooms separately, then arrange them sparingly on top of the meat before serving.

Fillet (tenderloin) steak rags with horseradish-blackberry dipping sauce

The combination of raw meat and acidic fruit is delicious. Keep the dish seasonal by varying the fruit as the year progresses, trying loganberries or mulberries in summer. I have added horseradish to this dipping sauce, but experiment with mustard and other spicy condiments instead. Make the dipping sauce in advance; it will keep for a few days in the refrigerator.

Serves 8 small or 4 regular portions

For the dipping sauce

300g (10½oz/2 cups) blackberries, plus 100g (3½oz/⅔ cup) more to serve

1 tablespoon caster sugar

1–2 tablespoons finely grated horseradish, to taste

1 tablespoon wine vinegar, or to taste

2–3 teaspoons brandy, to taste

For the steak

400g (14oz) fillet (tenderloin) steak

sea salt flakes and freshly ground black pepper

1 tablespoon finely grated horseradish, or to taste, plus more to serve

handful of small edible flowers, petals, leaves or a few sprigs of herbs, according to season

Crush and sieve the blackberries in a mouli-légumes (food mill), or push them through a sieve with the back of a spoon. Put the purée into a pan with the sugar and horseradish, place over a medium heat and bring to the boil, then reduce by one-third. Push through a sieve once more. Add the vinegar and brandy and leave to cool.

When ready to serve, slice the steak thinly and divide among individual plates.

Finely chop any meat trimmings to create a tartare, season with salt, pepper and a dab of horseradish and mix lightly with 1 tablespoon of the dipping sauce. Place a small pile of these trimmings on each serving of carpaccio and garnish with a whole blackberry and a couple of edible flowers, or a sprig of herbs.

Pour the dipping sauce into shot glasses or small bowls and put on the side of each plate. Sprinkle the meat with sea salt flakes and serve straight away.

VARIATIONS: Use Worcestershire, Tabasco or other spicy sauce instead of finely grated horseradish.
If you don't have fresh horseradish, use ready-made. Use raspberries, tayberries and so on according to what is in season. Experiment with venison, rabbit, lamb and kid fillets.

Wagyu with burdock and lotus root

The inspiration for this dish was my favourite breakfast salad at the Ginza, Mitsui Garden Hotel, in Tokyo. Both lotus and burdock root were new to me as ingredients, so imagine my delight at finding them back home at a Japanese supplier. Wagyu can be bought pre-sliced, a blessing given its high price ticket. If lotus roots and burdock elude you, substitute 1–2 sweet potatoes and 1 bunch of thick local asparagus spears respectively.

Serves 4 as a starter (appetizer)

For the beef and salad

1–2 lotus roots

salt

2 burdock roots

3 tablespoons rapeseed (canola) oil

1 teaspoon sake

1 teaspoon mirin

1 teaspoon soy sauce

150g (5½oz) paper-thin ready-sliced chilled wagyu

For the dressing

100ml (3½fl oz/scant ½ cup) extra virgin olive oil

juice of 1 lemon

1 garlic clove, crushed

1 tablespoon anchovy sauce, or mashed anchovy, or French mustard

sea salt flakes and freshly ground black pepper

Scrub the lotus roots carefully, so as not to bruise or damage them. Immerse in a pan of cold salted water over a medium-high heat and boil until tender, say 20–30 minutes, depending on size. Test for doneness with the point of a sharp knife; they should be tender all the way through. Drain, cool, then slice thinly.

Put all the ingredients for the dressing in a screw-top jar, seal and shake well. Set aside.

Scrub the burdock roots, immerse in cold water and cut into 3cm (1¼in) lengths. Place a wok over a high heat, adding the rapeseed oil and the burdock root pieces and stir-fry, adding a good pinch of salt. Turn once, then add the sake, mirin and soy sauce. Fry for about 5 more minutes, then transfer the burdock to a plate and leave to cool. Deglaze the wok with 50ml (1¾fl oz/scant ¼ cup) water and pour over the lotus root slices.

When both the lotus and burdock roots have cooled, cut the wagyu into 12 x 5 x 3cm (4½ x 2 x 1¼in) rectangles and roll each piece of burdock root in a rectangle of meat. Chill.

Arrange 3 slices of lotus root on each serving plate, or serve on a large platter and let everyone help themselves. Put a burdock and wagyu roll in the middle of each piece of lotus root and serve with the dressing, shaking it first, to emulsify once again.

Tartare

I have always loved a steak tartare and go out of my way to eat it when I am in France. But I was delighted to discover recently that it is also popular in Germany, where it is served with rye bread. Try it, they are made for each other! You will find the French and German versions here, along with a couple of my own inventions.

The word 'tartare' is often used to describe any raw meat, fish or vegetable dish in which the principal ingredient is chopped up or minced (ground) rather than sliced. The finished tartare is either hand-shaped into a doughnut shape, fashioned into quenelles with two large spoons, or shaped with tian moulds and served on a decorated plate.

The origins of what is generally accepted as a French speciality – steak tartare – are unclear, but we do know that it was a popular dish in Germany as far back as the Middle Ages. German immigrants introduced the dish, along with hamburgers and other iconic dishes, to North America, giving rise to tartare's other name, *biftek à l'Américaine*. It is not unreasonable to suppose that the genre was originally German, as raw meat dishes seem to have cropped up wherever the German diaspora landed. In Chile, German immigrants created what they called *crudos* (Spanish for 'raw') around the ranching communities. Some tartare

recipes also contain lime or lemon juice and jalapeño chillies, which would indicate some South American or Mexican cross-pollination of the recipe at some stage. What is certain is that there is no evidence whatsoever to suggest that tartare was originally created by the Tartars! This said, it is of course probable that they, just like other peoples, ate raw meat.

In France, steak tartare is made by mixing the chopped sirloin (short loin) steak (or horse meat) with raw egg, Worcestershire or Tabasco sauce and seasoning. Optional extras served alongside could include gherkins (dill pickles), capers, mayonnaise, various cheeses, herbs such as parsley, onion and garlic.

In Germany, *Tatar* is very much a summer dish and has two classifications: *Rindstatar*, made with beef, and *Schweinemett*, made with pork or a mixture of pork and beef. The former is a more expensive gourmet treat, the latter more workaday.

The flavourings for the meat vary according to region. Classically it is flavoured with raw egg and some salt and freshly ground white pepper, but garlic, caraway seeds and paprika are also traditional. Given the German love of gherkins (dill pickles), these can be served on the side.

Other global classic raw meat dishes

Thailand has its own raw beef recipe, *koi soi*, from the North Eastern Isaan area, made of finely chopped raw beef, fish sauce, chilli, lime juice and fresh herbs. Korean *yukhoe* (see page 100) is made with beef strips mixed with soy, rice wine, sesame oil and sesame seeds topped with egg yolk, green chilli strips and garlic. Sometimes a salad of leaves, and / or a julienne of onions and carrot are served stirred into the salad. Another Korean dish, *gan hoe*, is made with raw beef liver in a sauce of sesame oil and salt.

Left: Veal fillet
Opposite: Hand-mincing raw fillet (tenderloin) tail of beef for tartare

Classic steak tartare

This recipe is based on the definition in my copy of *Larousse Gastronomique*: 'à la tartare is the name given to minced beef steak seasoned with salt and pepper, re-shaped into a steak and served uncooked with a raw egg on top and on the side, capers, raw onion and parsley.' Importantly, the word for 'mince' in French (*hacher*) is most accurately translated as 'finely chopped'. Whatever you do, don't use a food processor to chop the meat... unless you want a sloppy mess.

Serves 4

400g (14oz) home hand-minced (hand-ground) lean sirloin (short-loin) steak (see recipe introduction), fridge-cold

sea salt flakes and freshly ground black pepper

1 shallot, finely chopped

3 tablespoons finely chopped flat leaf parsley leaves

2 tablespoons salted capers, rinsed, drained and chopped

4 fresh free-range egg yolks

Home-made mayonnaise, to serve (optional, see page 43)

Carefully and judiciously season the finely chopped steak with salt and pepper, taste and then shape into 4 flat rounds. Arrange each to the side of a serving plate. Push the back of a spoon into the centres to create craters for the egg yolks.

Mix the shallot and parsley in a small bowl and divide among the 4 plates, putting a neat heap on each. Divide the chopped capers in the same way.

Put an egg yolk in the hollow on top of each tartare and serve straight away, with Home-made mayonnaise if you like, and brown sourdough bread. A match made in heaven!

RAW AND RARE

Tartare: my way

This is my own tried-and-tested variation on the classic theme. Serve as a main course or a starter (appetizer) or — as in the photograph on the previous page — on tasting spoons nestling on a tray of ice, as a surprising and reviving canapé. Try playing with your favourite flavours, adding mustards, horseradish, ketchup and so forth. This recipe can also be adapted to include Japanese, South American or Thai flavourings, so create your very own mash-up tartare. Also try using other meats, such as venison, veal or kid.

Serves 8 as a starter (appetizer), or makes 30 tasting spoons

For the tartare

400g (14oz) home hand-minced (hand-ground) lean sirloin (short loin) steak, fridge-cold (see page 78)

1 large shallot, finely chopped

1½ tablespoons extra virgin olive oil

a few drops of Tabasco sauce; you know how spicy you like your food!

1½ tablespoons Worcestershire sauce

4 tablespoons finely chopped flat leaf parsley leaves, plus more for tasting spoons (optional)

4 cocktail gherkins (dill pickles), finely chopped

2 tablespoons salted capers, rinsed, drained and chopped

sea salt flakes and freshly ground black pepper

For tasting spoons

2 tablespoons mayonnaise (for home-made, see page 43)

For a starter (appetizer)

8 fresh quail's egg yolks

Put the meat in a bowl. Add the shallot, olive oil, Tabasco and Worcestershire sauces, the parsley, gherkins (dill pickles) and capers. Mix lightly, taste, then season with salt and pepper (you may not need salt if you have used salted capers). Add the mayonnaise (if using for tasting spoons) and mix the ingredients together well with your hands.

To make tasting spoons, fill each tasting spoon and round off the top neatly, by pressing lightly with an inverted spoon. Arrange on a bowl of crushed ice and serve straight away.

For a starter (appetizer), carefully shape 1 heaped tablespoon of the mixture, and turn it out on to the middle of a plate. Repeat twice more, making a trefoil arrangement. Using the back of a teaspoon, make an indentation in the centre and put the quail's egg yolk in it. Serve straight away.

VARIATION: For a main course, divide the mixture into 4 balls, then flatten the meat with the palm of your hands. Make an indentation on the top of each ball with the back of a spoon. Put a tartare to the side of each plate and serve with small neat individual piles of chopped gherkins (dill pickles), capers and mayonnaise. Top each tartare with a fresh free-range hen's egg yolk.

Kid fillet with parsley and pomegranate

If you have never eaten kid meat, you have a treat in store. It is delicate and sweet in flavour, tender in texture and delicious. The quality of the kid meat produced by my local supplier, Tregorras Farm, is so good – sweet and tender – that it would be a sin to slow-cook it. It should be seared briefly, or served raw. Kid is highly ethical meat as it comes from unwanted male goats produced by the goat's dairy industry, that would otherwise be killed at birth. It is low in fat and particularly rich in potassium and iron.

Serves 4 as a starter (appetizer), or makes about 22 tasting spoons

20g (¾oz/⅓ cup) finely chopped flat leaf parsley leaves

good pinch of sea salt flakes and ground pink peppercorns

300g (10½oz) kid fillets, finely chopped

1 tablespoon extra virgin olive oil

1 tablespoon pomegranate molasses

1 tablespoon pomegranate seeds, plus more to serve

2 limes, cut into wedges, to serve

Put the parsley in a bowl and add the salt and ground peppercorns, the chopped kid, oil and pomegranate molasses. Stir well, then add the pomegranate seeds and stir again.

Either divide into tasting spoons, or serve as a starter (appetizer) or main course, offering lime wedges on the side, and decorating with more pomegranate seeds.

La carne cruda all'albese

Follow the recipe quantities on page 85, home hand-mincing (hand-grinding) the rose veal rather than slicing it. About 30 minutes before serving, mix it with the oil, garlic, salt and pepper. Mix well, then add the lemon juice. Divide between tasting spoons and top each with a shaving of Parmesan, offering extra lemon juice for those who want it.

Makes about 25 tasting spoons.

Rindstatar or Schweinemett brochen

Spotting this tartare-on-rye open sandwich on sale at a service station in Germany made me realize just how embedded *Rindstatar* is in German food culture. Both chopped beef and pork — or a mixture — are used. (It is perfectly safe to eat uncooked pork in the West, now that tape worm has been eliminated.) The flavourings for the meat vary according to region. Classically it is flavoured with raw egg, some salt and white pepper, but garlic, caraway seeds and paprika are also traditional. Given the German love of gherkins, I like to add a few slices to each serving.

Makes 12 slices

400g (14oz) lean, tender steak, possibly sirloin (short loin) steak, or half sirloin (short loin) steak and half pork tenderloin

1 large garlic clove (optional)

2 heaped tablespoons Home-made mayonnaise (see page 43)

1 tablespoon paprika, or caraway seeds

1 teaspoon salt

freshly ground white pepper

softened butter, to serve

12 slices of dark rye bread, or pumpernickel, cut 1cm (½in) thick

2 small onions, thinly sliced

a few gherkins (dill pickles), thinly sliced (for home-made, see page 158)

Trim any fat or sinew from the meat and chop or hand-mince (hand-grind) it finely.

Cut the garlic clove in half and rub it around the inside of a mixing bowl. Add the chopped meat, the mayonnaise, paprika or caraway, salt and white pepper and mix with your hands. Taste and add more seasoning if you want.

Butter the rye bread and spread the chopped meat mixture on top, up to 1cm (½in) thick. Top with a couple of onion and / or gherkin (dill pickle) slices and serve.

Korean yukhoe beef strips with soy, sesame and chilli

This recipe is based on a Korean beef tartare; the beef is cut into strips, rather than chopped finely, then mixed with Asian seasonings and topped with an egg yolk. I like to add lime juice, but feel free to omit that if you want your yukhoe to be more authentic. Both are good!

Serves 8 small or 4 regular portions

400g (14oz) beef fillet (tenderloin) tails (see page 78)

6–8 spring onions (scallions)

1 chilli, deseeded (optional)

good pinch of chilli (red pepper) flakes

2 tablespoons soy sauce, plus a few drops more for the egg yolks

2 tablespoons toasted sesame oil

2 tablespoons rice wine

1 teaspoon sugar

juice of 2 limes (optional)

2 tablespoons toasted sesame seeds

pared zest of ½ unwaxed lime, cut into julienne, to serve

For a starter (appetizer)

8 fresh quail's egg yolks

For a main course

4 fresh free-range hen's egg yolks

Trim any fat or sinew from the meat. Slice the meat thinly and cut into 5mm (¼in) strips. This can be done up to 2 hours in advance; if so, cover and refrigerate.

Cut the spring onions (scallions) and chilli (if using) into julienne, then put in a bowl, cover and refrigerate.

When ready to serve, put the chilli (red pepper) flakes in a bowl with the 2 tablespoons of soy sauce, sesame oil, rice wine, sugar and lime juice (if using). Mix with a fork.

Put the quail's or hen's egg yolks (depending if using for a starter / appetizer or main course) in individual dipping bowls with a few drops of soy sauce and leave for 5 minutes.

Add the prepared steak to the marinade with half the sesame seeds and mix lightly. Add the spring onion (scallion) mixture and mix lightly again.

Serve in individual bowls, with the egg yolk, sprinkled with the remaining sesame seeds and a few strands of julienned chilli and lime zest. Guests can add and mix in the marinated egg yolk themselves.

VARIATION: Try experimenting with this recipe Thai-style, adding fish sauce, more chilli and herbs.

Seared

Seared meat dishes make great main courses for family meals and supper and lunch parties, especially in summer when lighter dishes are the order of the day. The meats are marinated or coated in advance, then seared on a white-hot griddle or in a super-hot oven, sliced thickly and served artfully decorated, with vegetables or salad.

Fillets are lean and tender and their diminutive girth makes them perfect for rapid cooking. For those dissenters who prefer their meat well-cooked (perish the thought), simply return a few slices to the oven until cooked through. Fillet (tenderloin) of beef and cheaper fillet (tenderloin) tails are perfect (see page 78). Neck fillet of lamb (see page 110) is sinewy, but offers a delicious and cheap family meal.

Venison and wild boar fillets are quite small, only around 300g (10½oz) each, but the meat is solid, there is no waste and a fillet will feed four when served with plenty of vegetables, or after a generous starter (appetizer).

Kid or rabbit loin are exquisite but probably best served as a starter (appetizer), due to their diminutive size. With venison or wild boar, the eye of the loin or the cannon is a bigger piece of meat if you are feeding numbers, or want to create a wow factor for the festive season. Pork tenderloin would also work, but I confess I'm not a fan of pink pig.

Breast meat of game such as pheasant, pigeon, partridge and farmed duck (see page 112), marinated and seared in a pan, are delicious served pink. Lastly, a rather old-fashioned cut of beef called skirt in England, and bavette in France, can be marinated, rolled up and seared (see page 116). If you like experimenting, don't be afraid to mix and match any of the marinades and coatings in this chapter.

Game meat can only really be sourced from a local or specialist butcher or farm shop, and it is well worth cultivating your local butcher, not only because they will let you know when they have something special on offer, but also because they will sell top-quality local meat.

It is advisable to order specialist cuts, such as those used in this section, well in advance. There is little more disheartening than planning a menu and then finding that the meat you want is not available.

It is essential to heat a griddle over a high heat for 15–20 minutes before you sear any meat on it. The outside will sear quickly and be easy to roll over to sear on the next side when ready. There is no need to oil the griddle; whatever is cooking will self-release with a light poke from a fish slice. Always heat the oven to its maximum temperature before putting the meat in the hottest part of it, and turn it once it has seared on one side. Don't attempt to griddle meat with a coating on, as it will burn. Coated meat such as the beef skirt and venison here (see pages 116 and 118) should be cooked in the hottest part of the oven.

These dishes can be prepared in advance and cooked last minute. However do remember that any accompanying roast vegetables will probably need to be in the oven longer than the meat, and therefore need to be started earlier.

Left: Miso oven-seared rolled skirt with marinade (see page 116)
Opposite: The skirt tied for searing

Tamari soy fillet (tenderloin) tails with julienne of vegetables

This is the simplest and most successful combination of flavours with which to quick-cook any cut of beef, whether for stir-fry, roast, barbecue, griddle or grill (broiler). It also works a treat for tuna loin. If you have a traditional butcher, they are sure to have fillet (tenderloin) tails: the thin, pointed end of the fillet (tenderloin). These are tender and a cheaper alternative to the fillet (tenderloin) 'proper' and — because of their narrow girth — are perfect for searing.

Serves 4

For the meat and marinade	For the vegetables	For the dressing
600g (1lb 5oz) fillet (tenderloin) tails	60g (2oz) sweet potato	2 teaspoons extra virgin olive oil
1 tablespoon extra virgin olive oil	60g (2oz) cucumber	2 teaspoons tamari soy sauce
1 tablespoon tamari soy sauce	30g (1¼oz) spring onion (scallion) tops (the green parts)	2 teaspoons mirin
1 tablespoon mirin		2 teaspoons lime juice
3 garlic cloves, peeled and cut into slivers		
1–2 teaspoons horseradish		

Trim any surface fat or sinew from the fillet (tenderloin) tails and put them in a large shallow dish.

Mix the oil, tamari, mirin, garlic and horseradish in a mug, whisk with a fork, then pour over the meat and marinate for 1 hour, turning the tails from time to time.

Meanwhile, peel the sweet potato and cut it into julienne. Julienne the cucumber (do not peel) and the spring onion (scallion) tops and immerse them all in ice-cold water until required.

Put the dressing ingredients in a salad bowl and whisk to emulsify them.

When ready to serve, heat a griddle pan over a high heat until white-hot. Put a serving dish and plates in a warm oven. Drain the julienne of vegetables thoroughly and leave to dry in a clean folded tea towel.

Drain off the marinade from the meat and discard. Sear the steak on the griddle, to your liking. Tails are usually quite thin, and the griddle is very hot, so 1 minute on each side should be sufficient if you like rare steak. For medium, leave the meat for 2–3 minutes on each side. For well-done, leave it for 3–5 minutes.

Transfer to a chopping board and cut into 2cm (¾in) slices. Arrange on the warmed serving plate.

Put the julienne of vegetables in the bowl with the dressing and mix well. Pile the vegetables on top of the meat and serve at once.

Scattered sushi with seared beef, chopped broccoli 'blossoms' and shiitake

When we think of 'sushi' in the West, we think of nori rolls and nigiri, where raw fish is laid over the top of ovals of rice. However, in Japan, there are less-formal sushi dishes, known as 'scattered' sushi, where bite-sized pieces of raw fish or meat are scattered over a bowl of vinegared rice. (Sushi in fact refers to the preparation of the rice, rather than the shaping.)

The rice and vegetables can be prepared in advance (though don't chill the rice or it will toughen) and the toppings can be added when ready to serve. For the meat, make sure that you buy fillet (tenderloin) tails that will sear quickly (see page 78), and cut into lots of small, thin slices.

Serves 4

For the rice

300g (10½oz/1⅔ cups) Japanese short-grain sushi rice

4cm (1½in) square of kombu

40ml (1¼fl oz/⅙ cup) rice vinegar

40g (1½oz/⅙ cup) granulated sugar

2 teaspoons salt

For the vegetables

1 large bunch of spring onions (scallions)

150g (5½oz) Tenderstem broccoli

150g (5½oz) shiitake mushrooms

2–3 tablespoons cold-pressed rapeseed oil

3 garlic cloves, very finely chopped

3cm (1¼in) piece of root ginger, very finely chopped

2 tablespoons soy sauce

For the meat and marinade

350g (12oz) beef fillet (tenderloin) tail (see page 78)

1½ tablespoons sake

1½ tablespoons soy sauce

1½ tablespoons mirin

For the dipping sauce per person

4 tablespoons soy sauce

4 teaspoons mirin

To serve

Japanese pickles, for home-made try Rice vinegar pickled samphire (salicornia) (see page 150)

wasabi

sushi pickled ginger

Start with the rice. Wash it in 2–3 changes of cold water until it runs clean, then leave it to drain in a sieve for 1 hour.

Put the rice in a deep pan, add 400ml (13fl oz/1⅔ cups) water and the kombu, place over a medium heat, cover and bring gently to the boil. Once boiling, discard the kombu. Cover, increase the heat and boil hard for 1 minute. Shake the pan, then reduce the heat to low and simmer gently until all the water has been absorbed, say 15 minutes, but check from time to time. Switch off the heat and uncover, then cover the pan with a clean folded cloth and replace the lid, wrapping the cloth over the lid. Leave the rice to stand over the switched-off heat for another 15 minutes.

Meanwhile, put the vinegar, sugar and salt in a small pan and bring gently to simmering point, stirring from time to time to dissolve the sugar. Pour into a shallow bowl and leave to cool.

Transfer the rice to a large, shallow non-metallic bowl to cool. It is essential not to squash the rice and to keep the grains separate. Using a spatula or wooden spoon, toss the rice gently, fanning it with your other hand, adding the cooled vinegar mixture a little at a time during this process. You may not need to use it all; you don't want it to become mushy. The rice should be used the same day, but should not be refrigerated, or it will toughen.

Now for the vegetables. Chop the whites of the spring onions (scallions) very finely and cut the dark green tops into very fine rounds.

Pull the 'blossoms' of the broccoli from the stems and divide or chop into tiny florets. Tear or chop the shiitake into tiny pieces.

Heat a wok over a high heat for 60 seconds, add the oil and stir-fry the garlic, ginger and spring onion (scallion) whites until the aromas start to rise, then add the mushrooms and stir-fry for a minute or so. Now add the soy sauce, stir, then add the broccoli blossoms. Stir-fry for a few minutes, then turn once, add the spring onion (scallion) greens, turn once more, then take off the heat. Transfer to a shallow serving dish to cool.

Prepare the meat. Trim any fat or sinew from the beef fillet (tenderloin) and arrange the meat in a shallow dish. Pour over the sake, soy sauce and mirin and marinate for 1 hour; turning occasionally.

When ready to serve, heat a ridged griddle pan over a high heat until white-hot (for about 15 minutes).

Drain off the marinade from the meat and discard. Sear the steak on the griddle on each side until stripy. The griddle is very hot, therefore 1 minute on each side should be more than sufficient for rare meat. For medium, reduce the heat once seared and cook for 2–3 minutes on each side. For well-done, cook for 3–5 minutes on each side. Transfer the meat to a chopping board and cut into very thin slices.

Mix together the ingredients for the dipping sauce and place into 4 bowls.

Lightly and evenly mix the rice and vegetables together and spoon into individual bowls. Arrange the sliced meat over the top. Serve with the dipping sauce, Japanese pickles, wasabi and sushi pickled ginger.

VARIATION: Instead of beef (tenderloin) fillet, try wagyu, kid or rabbit fillets, or even tuna loin (again, make sure you buy a long thin piece that will sear quickly).

Seared lamb with fennel seeds and lemon juice

Neck fillet of lamb is not always easy to find. Your butcher may prefer to leave the cut as an integral part of the shoulder joint, rather than cutting it out and 'spoiling' the shoulder. It is therefore often easier to find in a supermarket, or from a butcher that sells imported lamb neck fillets. It should be an inexpensive cut. It is fattier than other fillets and has some sinew running through it, but it is delicious nonetheless. Serve as a starter (appetizer), or a light main with a Fennel and orange salad with cocoa nibs (see page 137), or — for a more substantial meal — with braised Puy lentils and stir-fried cherry tomatoes.

Serves 4

2 x 250g (9oz) neck fillets of lamb

30g (1¼oz) fennel fronds, or flat leaf parsley leaves

5 garlic cloves

1 small red chilli, deseeded

2 heaped tablespoons fennel seeds

2 teaspoons sea salt flakes

2 teaspoons mixed peppercorns

extra virgin olive oil

2 lemons, cut into wedges

Trim the lamb fillets of any fat, sinew or skin, shaping the meat into as even a sausage shape as possible.

Chop the fennel or parsley, garlic and chilli together finely and put in a bowl. Crush the fennel seeds, salt and peppercorns in a mortar and pestle, then add to the chopped ingredients.

Lay a piece of cling film (plastic wrap) on a chopping board and tip half of this fennel mixture in the centre, creating a rectangle the length and circumference of the first neck of lamb. Roll a lamb fillet in it, pressing until the meat is well covered, then roll it up in the cling film (plastic wrap) and freeze for 2 hours. Repeat with the other neck fillet and chopped ingredients.

When ready to serve, heat a frying pan (skillet) large enough to contain both neck fillets over a medium-high heat until very hot. Add enough extra virgin olive oil to cover the base of the pan and add the neck fillets. Fry, turning, until golden all over. This should take 5 minutes for rare, 10 minutes for medium, or 15 for well-done. (Reduce the heat to medium if cooking for longer than 5 minutes.) Try not to over-cook the lamb, whatever your preference; remember that the lemon juice you add upon serving will further 'cook' the meat. Meanwhile, put a serving dish and plates in a warm oven.

Transfer the meat to a chopping board and slice. Arrange on plates and squeeze lemon juice over it all, or serve the lemon wedges on the side of the plates for each person to help themselves. Scatter any of the lamb's crust from the pan, which may have fallen off the meat, over the slices. Serve on warmed plates.

Cebiche of seared duck breast with seasonal vegetables

Cebiche of duck breast is a traditional Peruvian dish but, surprisingly, the authentic recipe is not served raw or even rare. My version is very definitely rare. Duck breast lends itself perfectly to being seared and served pink in the middle. Vary the cooking time according to how rare you like yours, but remember the citrus juice at the end will 'cook' it further and render it less pink. To serve as a starter (appetizer), use half the quantity of duck, leave to cool after cooking and slice thinly; serve with leaves instead of vegetables.

Serves 4

2 duck breasts, halved, total weight 500g (1lb 2oz)

2 unwaxed limes

2 small unwaxed oranges

ground cinnamon

cayenne pepper

sea salt flakes

500g (1lb 2oz) violet potatoes, or other waxy potatoes

12 young heritage carrots

100g (3½oz/3 cups) beetroot tops, or spinach leaves, curly kale, or other greens

extra virgin olive oil

toasted black and white sesame seeds (optional)

Prepare the duck breasts at least 30 minutes before cooking. Dry them thoroughly on kitchen paper (paper towels). Finely zest the limes and oranges and mix them together. Sprinkle the duck breasts lightly with a pinch each of cinnamon, cayenne and salt. Divide the grated citrus zest between the duck breasts and rub this and the spices into the meat, then put on a plate and cover loosely until required.

Scrub the potatoes and carrots and immerse the greens in cold water, then shake well and leave to drain. Put serving plates and dishes in a warm oven to heat.

Drop the potatoes into cold salted water, bring to the boil and simmer until tender, say 20 minutes. Test with the point of a knife to see if they are tender. Take care not to over-cook violet potatoes, or they will disintegrate in the water. Strain, put in a dish, cover and keep hot.

Tip the carrots into cold salted water in a pan that will fit underneath a steamer. Bring to the boil and simmer until tender, say 6–10 minutes, according to taste. Strain, put in a dish, cover and keep hot.

Put a heavy-based frying pan (skillet) over a medium-high heat. When it is hot, add the duck breasts, skin side down and cook for 2–4 minutes, then turn and cook on the other side for 2–4 minutes (2 minutes on each side will give rare meat; 4 minutes medium-rare). When it is ready, put it on a plate to keep hot.

Put the greens in a steamer basket and steam for 1–2 minutes over the carrots, or until tender. Tip on to a sheet of kitchen paper (paper towels) to soak up any excess water and then transfer to warmed dishes. Drizzle with extra virgin olive oil. Cover and keep hot.

Once all the vegetables are ready, cut the carrots in half lengthways and splash with a little extra virgin olive oil. Cut the potatoes in half and splash them, too, with oil. Arrange on warmed plates in separate piles.

Cut the duck breasts into 1cm (½in) slices and arrange with the vegetables on a serving platter, squeezing over each the juice of ½ lime and ½ orange. Serve at once, sprinkled with sesame seeds, if you like.

Cambodian seared duck breast with red cabbage slaw

This is a great dish for a party. The dressing and the salad can be made ahead of time and the duck breast cooked at the last minute. The quantity of sugar used in many Far Eastern salad dressings seems huge, but you will need it all. I have experimented with traditional recipes, both omitting and reducing the large amounts of palm sugar, but the flavours in the dressing just do not pull together without the sweetness.

Serves 8 small or 4 regular portions

For the dressing

3 large chillies, halved, deseeded and sliced

10 garlic cloves, peeled and crushed

3 tablespoons palm sugar

1 teaspoon sea salt

1 tablespoon fish sauce

1½ tablespoons white wine vinegar

1½ tablespoons lime juice

250ml (8½fl oz/1 cup) cold water

For the slaw

100g (3½fl oz/⅔ cup) shelled peanuts

100g (3½oz) green beans

¼ red cabbage, finely sliced

¼ white cabbage, finely sliced

1 green (bell) pepper, finely sliced

1 shallot, red if possible, finely chopped

6 garlic cloves, finely chopped

handful of Thai or regular basil leaves

handful of mint leaves, torn

handful of parsley leaves, finely chopped

1–2 red chillies, deseeded and cut into julienne

pared zest of 1 unwaxed lime, cut into julienne

For the duck

vegetable oil

240g (8½oz) duck breast

Make the dressing in advance: put all the ingredients into a blender and work until smooth. Transfer to a screw-top jar, seal the lid and store in the fridge until required.

To roast the peanuts, put them in a wok over a medium heat and keep flipping them until they turn golden. Do not be tempted to leave them to their own devices; they will burn for sure. When brown, take the wok outside and toss the peanuts in the air a few times; most of the peanut skins will float away. Leave to cool, then put in a plastic bag and crush evenly with a rolling pin.

Drop the green beans into a pan of boiling water, then return to the boil and simmer for 1 minute. Scoop out with a slotted spoon and plunge them into a bowl of iced water, then drain.

Prepare all the vegetables and herbs, set aside the julienned chillies and lime zest, and arrange the rest of the vegetables and herbs in a large salad bowl.

When ready to serve, put a frying pan (skillet) over a high heat, add enough vegetable oil to cover the base and add the duck to the pan. Brown quickly all over, then transfer to a chopping board and slice thinly.

Add three-quarters of the dressing to the salad, add the duck slices and toss well. Garnish with the julienned chilli and lime zest. Pour the remaining dressing over the top and scatter with the crushed nuts.

VARIATION: Try this recipe with seared fillet (tenderloin) steak, or even tuna loin.

Miso oven-seared rolled skirt with roasted pumpkin and turnips

Skirt or bavette steak is a rectangular, flat cut of beef from the diaphragm area, used traditionally in Cornish pasties and in Mexican fajitas. It is succulent, full of flavour and responds well to marinades and searing in a very hot oven. Red miso imparts a rich, umami flavour to the meat, making this a perfect summer roast, served hot and thickly sliced with vegetables, or cold and thinly sliced with a salad of rocket (arugula) and strawberries.

Serves 4

For the marinade and meat

100ml (3½fl oz/scant ½ cup) red miso

4 garlic cloves, peeled and crushed

2 tablespoons mirin

2 tablespoons sake

1 tablespoon finely chopped candied stem (preserved) ginger

1 tablespoon ginger syrup, from the stem (preserved) ginger jar

1 tablespoon extra virgin olive oil, plus more for the roasting tin

whole piece of skirt or bavette steak, 500-750g (1lb 2oz-1lb 10oz)

To serve

1 small butternut squash, or 2 heads of broccoli

500g (1lb 2oz) baby turnips or salad potatoes

1 tablespoon sesame oil

1 tablespoon sesame seeds (optional)

salt

Put the marinade ingredients in a screw-top jar, seal and shake well.

Lay the steak flat in a large shallow dish, pour the marinade over the top and leave for 1 hour (see page 102 for a photo), turning once during that time. Take the meat out of the marinade, roll it up as tightly as possible and tie it securely with kitchen string. (Be warned, this is a messy, but worthwhile job.) Return it to the marinade and turn to coat the meat evenly.

Preheat the oven to its maximum setting.

You'll probably have to cook the vegetables first. In winter, cut the squash into thin wedges and put in a roasting tin with the turnips. Add the sesame oil, toss and cook in the hot oven for 30-40 minutes, until golden and tender. Transfer to a warmed serving dish. In spring and summer, put the potatoes in cold salted water, bring to the boil and simmer until tender, say 20 minutes (reserve the water). At the same time, cut the broccoli into spears and cook for 4 minutes in lightly salted boiling water. Drain the broccoli and return it to the pan over a low heat, tossing with the sesame oil and sesame seeds.

Meanwhile, when ready to cook the meat, put it into a small oiled roasting tin with 2 tablespoons of water. Discard the excess marinade; do not be tempted to serve it with the meat, it is too rich and heavy. Cook in the oven for 20 minutes, then rest for 10 minutes for very pink meat; or cook for 30 minutes and rest for medium-rare; or cook for 40 minutes and rest for well-done. Meanwhile, warm serving plates and dishes.

When the cooking time for the meat and vegetables is up, put the meat on a chopping board and deglaze the roasting tin with 2-3 tablespoons boiling water (use the water the vegetables were cooked in, when you have it). Toss the potatoes (if using) in the pan juices.

Cut off and discard the string, then slice the meat into 8-12 thick slices and arrange on the warmed serving plate with the vegetables.

Seared venison with pomegranate jewels

The return of game to the table each autumn (fall) is always a treat, and meats such as wild boar and venison conjure up feasts of yore. But game dishes need not be heavy. Venison makes a beautiful-but-light dish to serve for a special occasion, with pomegranate jewels creating a festive finish; be sure to order it from your butcher in advance. I have only given cooking times for rare or medium-rare meat, as venison becomes very dry and dull when overcooked. Start preparations well ahead, to allow for freezing time.

Serves 8 as a main course with vegetables

800g–1kg (1lb 12oz–2¼lb) cannon of loin of venison, or 2 fillets of venison, each 200–300g (7–10½oz)

5 generous tablespoons pink peppercorns

2 tablespoons thyme leaves

50g (1¾oz/scant 1 cup) finely chopped flat leaf parsley leaves

finely chopped zest of 2 large unwaxed oranges

2 teaspoons sea salt flakes

3 tablespoons pomegranate molasses, plus more to serve

1 large or 2 small pomegranates

a little vegetable oil, for the baking tray

micro-herbs, petals and leaves, to serve (optional)

Trim the venison, removing any sinew or fat. Fold the skinny tail end of the fillets back on themselves (if using) to create an even shape.

Crush the peppercorns in a mortar and pestle and put in a bowl with the thyme, parsley, orange zest and salt and mix lightly. Lay a long piece of cling film (plastic wrap) (more than long enough to wrap the meat) on a work surface, tip the peppercorn mixture in the middle and spread it out to make a rectangle the same length and circumference as the meat (prepare 2 of these if cooking 2 fillets). Coat the meat in the pomegranate molasses, then roll it in the peppercorn mixture to create a crust all over. Seal it in the cling film (plastic wrap) and twist the ends. Keep in the fridge, then freeze for 2 hours just before cooking.

Meanwhile, scoop out the jewels from half the pomegranate and cut wedges from the rest. Wrap in cling film (plastic wrap) and set aside.

When the meat has been in the freezer for 2 hours, preheat the oven to its hottest setting. When the oven is up to temperature, unwrap the venison and lay it on an oiled baking tray. A cannon will need 20–30 minutes for rare meat, or 40 minutes for medium, turning once during cooking; fillets will need only half this time.

Leave to rest, covered, for 10 minutes before slicing, while you warm serving plates. Cut the meat into 1–2cm (½–¾in) slices. If, once sliced, you feel the meat is too pink, lay the slices back on the baking tray and return it to the hot oven for another 5 minutes. Arrange the sliced meat on warmed plates, drizzle with pomegranate molasses and sprinkle pomegranate jewels around. Decorate with the micro-herbs, petals and leaves, and top each serving with a thin wedge of pomegranate.

VARIATION: Use fillets of wild boar or kid as a starter (appetizer), or fillet (tenderloin) steak as a main.

Salads, vegetables
and dressings

Getting started: fruits and vegetables

Seasonal vegetables — raw or cooked, grown at home, locally, on a smallholding, organically or large scale — bring with them variety, vitamins, minerals, colour, texture and flavour to everyday eating. Vegetables and salad goods served raw — summer and winter, whole, sliced, chopped or grated — give an extra touch of vitality.

We hear so much about 'superfoods', but I believe that all vegetables and fruits are, in their own ways, superfoods. Ginger and other spices are strong antiseptics, kill germs and are natural effective medicines. Vegetables contain dietary fibre, which maintains healthy intestines. Many nuts contain essential minerals; Brazil nuts contain selenium which many of us lack in our diet; walnuts contain anti-ageing ingredients for the brain. The important thing is variety, to eat a little of everything so that body and mind can revel in the full bounty that nature has to offer.

Eating raw vegetables, fruit, nuts and seeds enhances not only their goodness, but also our enjoyment of fresh produce. The experience of colour, texture, sweetness and flavour are all notably heightened when produce is eaten just-picked, freshly prepared and raw.

There have never been more fresh vegetables on sale. Exotic produce is on offer year round. Polytunnels and glasshouses have extended the growing season of so much local produce and, because of this, many of us have lost touch with the seasons. Once upon a time the arrival of the new season's vegetables and fruit was greeted with such excitement... but now it passes unnoticed by many.

Eating fresh produce, raw or cooked, helps reduce the risk of cardiovascular disease, stroke, cancer and macular degeneration, due to its antioxidant and fibre content. Current recommendations suggest we should all be eating at least 80g (3oz) of fruits and vegetables per day, and while a few of us eat more than that, sadly many more eat far less.

Seasonal local produce has far more flavour as well as more nutritional value. It is important in Japanese home cooking, *washoku*, that a sense of season is reflected in everyday meals, and we too should take note. In Japan, it is believed that when produce first comes into season it is particularly important to the diet. So much so that it has given rise to the saying, 'Eating *hatsumono* (the new season's fare) extends life by 75 days,' and this may be true, as young produce is particularly high in vitamin C and in enzymes.

It is also believed in Japan that people's health is best supported by the land, water courses and sea on which they live. It is thought that eating wild plants, mushrooms and crops grown locally helps to avoid illnesses and extends life.

Locally focused eating is referred to as *shindofuji* (body and land are not two). Many of us who grow our own, or who live in the country, know the truth in this.

Where is the pleasure in eating a tasteless strawberry in January, dull asparagus in December, tough runner (string) beans in February? Eating should be a pleasure, and part of that enjoyment is connecting with the land and the people who produce our food. Take time to shop locally at your independent shops and stalls on the high street or the market, at a farm gate or in a farmer's market. Feel the excitement of seasonal shopping. The supermarket has its place, but buying everything under one roof to fill up a trolley encourages waste... and is no pleasure.

Make sure, when you are buying vegetables, that they are fresh. In season, buy root vegetables with their greens intact. Tomatoes and cucumbers should be firm and have the scent of the greenhouse about them (if a cucumber is wrapped in plastic, unwrap it). If vegetables are muddy, they are probably organic. Everything should have that freshly picked look about it. The produce should speak to you. Leaves should be stored in the fridge, tomatoes out of it, root vegetables in a cool cupboard in the dark.

A salad should not need a recipe; it can be as simple as a few leaves with olive oil and lemon juice. It can also be multi-layered, with raw and cooked vegetables, fruits, nuts, seeds, herbs, raw, cured and cooked meat, fish and cheese. The important thing is to always keep a small selection of salad goods and a jar of home-made dressing in your fridge.

Choose from Cos (Romaine), Little Gem and the ubiquitous Iceberg lettuces, which are sweet, crisp and keep well. Add a little peppery bitterness with rocket (arugula), watercress or dandelion leaves, or milder leaves such as lamb's lettuce or baby spinach. Add cool, fresh, juicy, crunch: (bell) peppers, celery, cucumber, kohlrabi, fennel, radish or carrot will do the trick. Leftover or lightly cooked vegetables add richness, and diced fruit vibrancy. Finish with an aromatic herb, such as basil, mint or parsley; radiant flowers such as rose petals, borage, nasturtium or pansy; seeds such as sunflower or pumpkin; and nuts such as pistachio or walnut. Toss with your dressing of choice... and you have a different salad for every day of the year.

'Cebiche' heritage tomatoes, sweetcorn and mint

This is a roller-coaster of lively, juicy flavours and the perfect accompaniment for grilled (broiled) meat and fish. Growers are increasingly experimenting with unusual varieties of tomatoes, grown for taste rather than looks. Heritage tomatoes come in a mishmash of shapes and colours. To show off the colours to best effect in this recipe, keep each separate. Buy your corn on the cob as fresh as possible, or even pick your own, then peel off the leaves and cut the corn kernels away with a knife. Their natural crunch and vibrant colour make them an ideal addition to any salad.

Serves 4 as a side salad

1 sweetcorn cob

500g (1lb 2oz) heritage tomatoes, ideally in mixed colours

juice of 1 lime

3 tablespoons extra virgin olive oil

½–1 habanero chilli, or other chilli, deseeded and finely chopped

handful of mint leaves, or parsley or coriander (cilantro) leaves, finely chopped, plus a few sprigs to serve

½ teaspoon sea salt flakes

Prepare this salad just before serving. Cut the corn kernels from the cob and pile them in the centre of a serving platter.

Cut the tomatoes into 1–2cm (½–¾in) cubes, keeping each colour separate, and arrange in separate piles around the corn.

Squeeze over the lime juice and sprinkle with the oil, chilli and chopped herbs. Scatter with salt and serve with the chopped herb sprigs.

VARIATION: Mix the chopped tomatoes in a bowl and add leftover cold meat, such as beef, venison or lamb, cut into bite-sized pieces, for a lunchtime main course dish.

Celeriac (celery root) salad with horseradish

This is a handy standby, as it keeps well in the fridge in an airtight container and can be made in advance. Be careful not to overdo the mayonnaise or it will be sickly. I keep it light by diluting the mayonnaise and adding oil. Serve with cured and smoked fish and meats as a starter (appetizer), or as a side salad.

Serves 4–6 as a side salad

500g (1lb 2oz) (1 small) celeriac (celery root)

juice of 1 large lemon

3–4 spring onions (scallions), white parts only, finely chopped, plus more to serve

6 cocktail gherkins (dill pickles), finely chopped

1 tablespoon creamed horseradish

150ml (5fl oz/⅔ cup) mayonnaise (for home-made see page 43)

50ml (1¾fl oz/scant ¼ cup) extra virgin olive oil

sea salt flakes and freshly ground black pepper

Either shred the celeriac (celery root) in a food processor, or grate it by hand. Put in a large bowl, add the lemon juice straight away (this stops the celeriac [celery root] turning brown) and mix lightly with a couple of forks, lifting the grated celeriac (celery root). Add the spring onions (scallions), gherkins (dill pickles) and horseradish and mix again.

Dilute the mayonnaise with 50ml (1¾fl oz/scant ¼ cup) warm water and add to the celeriac (celery root). Pour in the oil and mix again lightly with the forks. Add salt and pepper to taste, sprinkle with spring onion (scallion) and serve.

Shredded daikon and carrot with double sesame

Daikon is a snowy white giant radish, sometimes sold as 'mooli'. It has a strong peppery radish-like flavour and a crisp texture. Nothing else is quite like it, but, if you can't get hold of it, use grated kohlrabi. Once shredded, immerse the daikon in ice-cold water for 10 minutes, then drain and squeeze out the excess water before use; this reduces the strong taste.

Serves 4 as a side salad

For the vegetables

1 cucumber

1 large piece of daikon / mooli (about 250g/9oz), peeled and finely shredded

1 large carrot (about 250g/9oz), peeled and finely shredded

1–2 teaspoons toasted white sesame seeds

1–2 teaspoons black sesame seeds

For the dressing

2 teaspoons mirin

2 teaspoons tamari soy sauce

2 teaspoons toasted sesame oil

Partially peel, halve and deseed the cucumber, then put cut sides down on kitchen paper for 10 minutes to drain. Immerse the shredded daikon in iced water for 10 minutes, then drain and dry thoroughly.

Put the mirin, tamari and sesame oil in a screw-top jar, seal and shake. Dry the cucumber and finely slice. Put in a bowl with the carrot and daikon, mix well, then mix in the dressing. Sprinkle with the seeds.

Sweet summer vegetable salad with oriental dressing

The dressing for this salad is Japanese; use it sparingly to enhance the flavour of the new season's vegetables, rather than coating them. Try and source finger-sized courgettes (zucchini); their texture is rich and waxy, rather than pithy. If you grow your own, make sure you pick them when young. Buy local asparagus rather than imported spears. Broad beans (fava beans) must always be picked young, or they will be tough.

Serves 4 as a side salad

For the dressing

3 teaspoons mirin

3 teaspoons yuzu juice, or lemon juice

½ teaspoon honey

6 mint leaves, shredded

2 teaspoons sake

2 teaspoons tamari soy sauce

For the salad

150g (5½oz) young tender asparagus spears, trimmed

150g (5½oz) young, finger-sized courgettes (zucchini)

150g (5½oz) young broad beans (fava beans), podded

40g (1½oz/⅓ cup) firm raspberries, halved

toasted sesame oil, to serve

mint sprigs or courgette (zucchini) flowers, to serve (optional)

Put the dressing ingredients in a screw-top jar, seal and shake.

Slice the asparagus and the courgettes (zucchini) on the diagonal. Put in a salad bowl, add the broad beans (fava beans), the raspberries and dressing, mix well and add a drizzle of sesame oil.

Top with mint sprigs or courgette (zucchini) flowers, when available.

RAW AND RARE

Watercress, curly kale and pear mayonnaise with walnuts

Great care should be taken when buying shelled walnuts. They should look bright and golden brown, not dark and withered. Check the sell-by date and make sure there are six months or more before it expires: fresh walnuts are sweet and well-rounded in flavour; stale nuts are bitter. If you can, buy them from a local Middle Eastern store, where they will generally be very fresh and relatively inexpensive.

Serves 4 as a side salad

75-100g (2¾-3½oz/1-1⅓ cups) curly kale

1 heaped tablespoon mayonnaise (for home-made, see page 43)

2 tablespoons extra virgin olive oil

sea salt flakes and freshly ground black pepper

2 large ripe-but-firm William pears

juice of 1 lemon

50g (1¾oz/scant ½ cup) broken walnut pieces, plus more to serve

75-100g (2¾-3½oz/2-3 cups) watercress, torn into manageable pieces

Shred the kale finely in a food processor.

Put the mayonnaise in a salad bowl and stir in the oil; if it is very thick, add 1 tablespoon of hot water to dilute it. Taste and season accordingly.

Peel the pears, cut into slivers and toss in the lemon juice to stop them turning brown. Add to the mayonnaise sauce.

Roughly crush the walnuts in a freezer bag with a rolling pin, add to the pears and mix in lightly. All this can be done in advance.

When ready to serve, stir in the shredded kale.

Arrange the watercress on a serving platter and tip the pear salad into the middle. Serve topped with the extra crushed walnuts.

Crudités with tahini and lime dipping sauce

This dipping sauce was inspired by a Korean marinade for grilled (broiled) meat that is made by crushing sesame seeds with sesame oil to create a paste. I use ready-made tahini, which gives an easy-to-make and delicious dip. (Make sure you choose a good-quality, stone-ground tahini.)

If rainbow radishes are not available, use baby heritage carrots, or mix pink radishes with baby carrot, fennel and courgettes (zucchini), cutting them all into the same-sized sticks. Vegans may like to use this dipping sauce as a dressing for salads, rather than egg-based mayonnaise. Delicious!

Serves 4 as a starter (appetizer) or nibble

For the dipping sauce

2 generous dollops of light tahini paste (about 80g/3oz)

2 tablespoons vegetable oil

1 tablespoon light soy sauce

1 large garlic clove, lightly crushed, then halved lengthways (optional)

pinch of sea salt flakes, to taste (optional)

pinch of sugar, to taste (optional)

juice of 1 lime, plus lime wedges to serve

For the crudités

2 bunches of fridge-cold rainbow or pink radishes, or heritage carrots and other baby vegetables

Put the tahini in a bowl and beat in the vegetable oil and enough cold water to create a smooth paste; anything from 1–4 tablespoons. Add the soy sauce and the garlic (if using). Taste for seasoning and, if necessary, add the salt and sugar. Cover and store in the fridge until required (it keeps for about 1 week). If it curdles, simply add more water and beat until it comes right.

Pick over the radishes, carrots and other vegetables, trimming off any tired leaves and stalks. Cut large vegetables into diagonal slices or batons. Immerse in ice-cold water for 10 minutes or so until crisp, then drain and store in plastic bags in the fridge until required.

When ready to serve, add the lime juice to the dip. This may cause the dip to split, but don't worry, simply add 2–3 tablespoons of boiling water – or enough to dilute – and beat again, then decant into a serving bowl, or divide between individual dipping bowls (discard the garlic, if you used it).

Put the crudités in a bowl and serve with the dipping sauce and lime wedges.

Carpaccio of mushrooms with rocket (arugula) pesto

Use field, portobello or chestnut mushrooms here, or — for special occasions — porcini, if you are lucky enough to find any. Top them with finely chopped hard-boiled eggs before adding the rocket pesto, if you like. Serve as part of a mixed autumnal (fall) antipasto, or with bresaola or other cured meats.

Serves 4 as a side salad, or as a starter (appetizer) with cured meats

150g (5½oz) mushrooms

1½ lemons

80ml (2¾fl oz/⅓ cup) extra virgin olive oil

1 tablespoon Dijon mustard

sea salt and coarsely ground black pepper

handful of rocket (arugula) leaves

½ garlic clove

Wipe the mushrooms and slice them paper-thin. Put in a bowl and cover with cold water, add the juice of ½ lemon and leave for at least 1 hour, or overnight, until required. Put the oil, the juice of the remaining lemon and the mustard in a screw-top jar, add salt and pepper to taste, seal the lid and shake well.

When ready to serve, drain the mushrooms and dry carefully on kitchen paper, put them back in the bowl, add 1 tablespoon of the dressing and coat gently. Chop the rocket (arugula) and garlic very finely and add to the remaining dressing. Divide the mushrooms between plates or put them on a serving platter, spreading them out. Drizzle the rocket (arugula) pesto over the top and serve at once.

Fennel and orange salad with cocoa nibs

Fennel and orange is a classic Sicilian winter combination. I have added cocoa nibs to give it a new and rich dimension. The oranges will give up juice as you cut them, but pour it off and drink it rather than leaving it on the salad, otherwise the dressing will be too thin.

Serves 4 as a side salad

3 oranges

good pinch of ground cinnamon

1 large fennel bulb, thinly sliced lengthways, plus 2 teaspoons fennel fronds, finely chopped

sea salt flakes and freshly ground black pepper

2 tablespoons extra virgin olive oil

1 heaped teaspoon cocoa nibs, crushed

Peel the oranges with a sharp knife, cutting away the pith and the skin. Cut the peeled oranges into wedges or slices, then cut the slices in half and arrange them on a platter. Drink any excess juice. Sprinkle lightly with the cinnamon and scatter half the fennel fronds on top.

Cover the orange with the sliced fennel, adding salt and pepper. Drizzle with the oil and finish with the remaining fennel fronds and the crushed cocoa nibs. Serve at once.

Salsa of red onion, (bell) peppers and avocado with popcorn

Salsas make colourful, refreshing additions to any simple summer dish, such as grilled (broiled) or fried steak, burgers or fish, or can also revitalize winter leftovers. To turn this into a main course, add cooked and cooled quinoa, rice, chickpeas (garbanzo beans) or lentils, and extra dressing. Or turn the salsa out on to a bed of leaves and surround with prawns (shrimp), flaked salmon, mozzarella or feta. Or even add chopped raw fish to create a refreshing tartare.

This is a versatile dish and it's easy to vary the ingredients: try peas and sweetcorn; or cut tomatoes and cucumber in half, remove the seeds and drain on kitchen paper (paper towels) before cutting into tiny pieces. For sweetness, add ripe kiwis, peaches or plums, chopped small. For a little crunch, add seeds or dried banana chips.

Serves 4 as a side or starter (appetizer) salad

good handful of popping corn kernels

2 tablespoons rapeseed (canola) oil

sea salt flakes and freshly ground black pepper

1 red onion

1 lime

2 ripe avocados

1 large yellow (bell) pepper

1 large red (bell) pepper

handful of coriander (cilantro) leaves, torn

a few drops of Tabasco sauce, or to taste

2–3 tablespoons extra virgin olive oil

Put the popcorn in a saucepan with a lid and add the rapeseed (canola) oil. Cover with the lid and put over a medium-high heat. Gently shake the pan over the heat until the popping starts. When the popping becomes almost constant, slide the pan off the heat, wait a few seconds for the popping to stop, then carefully check under the lid to see if all the corn has popped. If there is still a lot of corn to pop, put it back on the heat. (There will always be a few 'dead men'.) Add salt and pepper and leave to cool.

Chop the onion and immerse in cold water for 10 minutes, then drain and dry on a clean tea towel.

Zest the lime with a potato peeler, chop the zest finely and wrap it in cling film (plastic wrap). This is to create a rough texture; using a zester would destroy the texture.

Chop the avocados into 1cm (½in) cubes and immediately squeeze the lime juice over. Chop the (bell) peppers the same size.

Put the diced (bell) peppers and avocado in a bowl with the onion. Add the coriander (cilantro) leaves, the lime zest and Tabasco sauce to taste (I like lots, but if you don't, just add 3–4 gentle shakes to bring out the flavour of the salsa without making it 'hot').

Season with salt and pepper and the olive oil. Mix well, then add most of the cooled popcorn, reserving a handful to sprinkle over the top.

Spring vegetable Macedonia with matcha dressing

Matcha is the tea served at the traditional Japanese tea ceremony. It is a bright pea green, ground powder-thin, has an unusual, bittersweet flavour and is high in antioxidants. Matcha is very popular in Japan, where it is used to flavour and colour a host of ice creams, biscuits (cookies) and cakes.

The combination of vegetables here lends itself to many of the other dressings in this chapter. The vegetables can be used raw, if you prefer, or blanched and dressed while still warm.

Serves 6 as a side salad

For the dressing

1 teaspoon matcha green tea powder

3 tablespoons rapeseed (canola) oil

pinch of sea salt flakes

juice of ½ lemon

For the vegetables

150g (5½oz/generous 1 cup) peas, ideally freshly podded

150g (5½oz/1 cup) young broad beans (fava beans), ideally freshly podded

150g (5½oz) baby carrots

150g (5½oz) tender young asparagus spears

small bag of baby leaf salad

6 cup-shaped Cos (Romaine) or radicchio leaves, to serve (optional)

To make the dressing, either put the matcha in a bowl with the oil and salt and mix with a traditional Japanese whisk (see photo, left), or put the matcha, oil and salt in a screw-top jar, screw on the lid and shake the jar until the dressing is smooth. Taste for seasoning, and adjust if necessary.

If blanching the vegetables, bring a pan of lightly salted water to the boil and blanch each type of vegetable separately for 1 minute, cooking the asparagus last. Drain and dry each thoroughly on a clean cloth. Cut the asparagus tips diagonally into 3cm (1¼in) pieces and reserve. Cut the asparagus stalks and carrots diagonally into bite-sized pieces and put in a mixing bowl. When all the vegetables are ready, and still warm, add half the dressing and all the lemon juice, then leave to cool completely.

If using raw vegetables, simply put the peas and broad beans (fava beans) in a bowl and cut the carrots and asparagus diagonally into bite-sized pieces, as before. Add half the dressing and all the lemon juice. Add the baby leaf salad and taste for seasoning.

Line a large serving plate with the cup-shaped Cos (Romaine) or radicchio leaves (if using), and spoon the salad into the middle, or into the 'cups' for individual servings. Splash the remaining dressing over all, or serve it on the side.

VARIATION: Use other combinations of young vegetables as the year unfolds.

Summer tri-colour beets with crushed Brazils, seeds and marjoram

If you can't find three colours of beets, use good old-fashioned purple baby beets. You can buy these ready-cooked, but you get better flavour and texture when you roast them yourself. Vary the nuts and seeds and, if you don't have marjoram in the garden, use thyme or rosemary instead.

When using mixed colour beets, take care not to stain the pale roots with the darker ones. If the beets are very small and tender, they can be scrubbed, cut into wedges and dressed raw.

Serves 4 as a side salad

500g (1lb 2oz) bunch of raw baby beets, ideally in mixed colours

extra virgin olive oil

sea salt flakes

6 sprigs of marjoram, thyme or rosemary, ideally with flowers, plus 4–6 more to serve

1–2 tablespoons pumpkin seeds, or other seeds

50g (1¾oz/¼ cup) Brazil nuts, or other nuts

Preheat the oven to fan 170°C/190°C/375°F/gas mark 5. Cut off the beet leaves and reserve them for salad if they are young and in good condition, or for steaming as a vegetable. Do not cut the beets, as they will bleed colour, but wash them; you may need a small brush to get rid of any soil. Dry thoroughly.

If the beets are very small and tender, scrub them, cut into wedges and dress raw with oil and salt. This should be done 24–48 hours in advance as the dressing softens them and eliminates the woody taste. Keep different colours separate, so as not to taint the pale beets with the juice of the purple ones.

If cooking, spread out a large piece of foil, pile the beets in the middle, add a drizzle of oil and the 6 sprigs of marjoram and seal the foil loosely around them. Put on a baking sheet and cook for 45–90 minutes, depending on size, or until tender. To check for doneness, open the packet and slide a knife into the centre of a beet; if it slides in and out easily they are ready. When cool enough to handle, separate the different coloured beets. Carefully peel them and cut into wedges. Again, peel and cut pale beets first, so as not to get a purple stain on them. Put each colour of beet in a different bowl.

Tip the pumpkin seeds on to a baking tray and roast in the same oven for 5 minutes, then shake and roast for another 5 minutes or until golden. Leave to cool. Store in an airtight jar and use as required. Meanwhile, put the Brazil nuts in a sturdy plastic bag and roughly crush with a rolling pin. Pick the leaves off the 4-6 herb sprigs to serve, discarding brown leaves and retaining a few delicate top sprigs. Chop the rest finely. (If the herbs are in flower, pick off the flowers and set aside.) Divide between the beet bowls, add 1 tablespoon of extra virgin oil and a few salt flakes to each and mix, then cover.

Carefully arrange the beets on a serving plate, start with the dark ones and finish with the light ones and grade the colours in between (taking care not to get dark beetroot stain on the light beets). Scatter with the roasted seeds, crushed Brazils and herb flowers or leaves. If the pile of beets is particularly pretty, just add a scattering of nuts and seeds and offer the rest on the side. Serve at once.

VARIATION: To make this into a light lunch or supper dish, before adding the nuts, seeds and so on, arrange small cubes of feta, tofu or goat's cheese around the beets.

Pickles

Pickles: a global love affair

Making pickles was once the only way of preserving fresh produce to enhance dull winter eating. But making and eating pickles remains as popular as ever, because pickles create flavours that complement and balance the foods they are served with. So much so that, today, most fine eateries make them in-house.

Pickling was once a necessity the world over. Where there were seasons, there was the need to preserve excess produce to keep people going through the lean times of the winter. Today, most of us enjoy the benefits of refrigeration, modern farming and access to a worldwide produce market... and theoretically preserving should be a thing of the past for all but the gardening brigade. However, we crave the myriad flavours that preserving creates. It seems that the more spare time modern technology affords us, the more inclined we are to fill it with back-in-the-day pursuits such as vegetable gardening and preserving.

In Japan, pickling is so important that there is a Tsukemono (pickle) Research Institute. Miso soup, rice and pickles once constituted a Japanese meal, breakfast included. Back then, pickles were essentials and everyone made their own but, today, their preparation is most often left to the professionals. Every region has its sought-after speciality, the souvenir of choice for Japanese travellers. Wild plants, farmed vegetables, fish and meat all receive the treatment. At the colourful Nishiki koji-dori market in Kyoto, diminutive wooden pickling barrels vie for floor space, while rows and rows of little sample bowls are set out for the customers. Simply pickle heaven!

Sweden is another pickle haven. The long, cold, dark winters and short growing season meant that ways of preserving produce had to be found. There is still a strong tradition for home preserving in a sweet-and-sour pickle, more often than not perfumed with dill (see page 158).

Northern Europe, the UK and the Mediterranean region all have their pickling traditions. I have included Italian specialities, preserved in wine, vinegar and water; British spiced treats pickled traditionally in cider or malt vinegar; and the ubiquitous gherkin (dill pickle), that crossed the Atlantic to America with the German diaspora and has now taken up permanent residence in pretty much every continent of the world. Unless you grow your own and are preserving to use up a glut, experiment with small quantities – say 500g (1lb 2oz) or so – and make a variety of pickles.

If you're making preserves, you will need to sterilize the lids and jars. Jars should be washed in hot soapy water, rinsed and inverted on a baking tray. Dry in a warm oven (at least fan 120°C/140°C/275°F/gas mark 1) for 20 minutes. Or put through the hot cycle of a dishwasher. Lids and rubber seals can be scalded with boiling water.

Opposite from left: La giardiniera primavera *of baby fennel (see page 149), Rice vinegar pickled samphire (salicornia) (see page 150), Mixed mushroom salad pickle (see page 154)*

RAW AND RARE

La giardiniera primavera

This sweet-and-sour mixed antipasto is made in many Italian households, especially in Southern Italy. There are no hard and fast rules; every cook has their own recipe and would argue it is the best. Choose any vegetables according to the season, but don't overcook them, as they should retain texture and colour. Large jars are best if you are pickling long pieces of veg. I used one-quarter each of aubergines (eggplants), finger courgettes (zucchini), cherry tomatoes and young carrots when developing this recipe, but you can use fennel, green beans, small onions, celery, (bell) peppers, asparagus, cauliflower... or anything else that takes your fancy, either as single types or as a mixed pickle.

Serve, drained, as part of an antipasto, with freshly chopped herbs and a drizzle of extra virgin olive oil. Or serve with cured meats, cheeses, olives and other Italian treats, or stir into salads.

Makes 1kg (2¼lb) jar or more, or equivalent smaller jars

250ml (8½fl oz/1 cup) white wine	1 small wine glass of extra virgin olive oil	1kg (2¼lb) vegetables (see recipe introduction)
250ml (8½fl oz/1 cup) white wine vinegar	1 teaspoon chilli flakes (optional)	12 garlic cloves
65g (2oz/⅓ cup) sugar	1 bay leaf	fennel fronds or flowers
65g (2oz/¼ cup) coarse sea salt	1 teaspoon juniper berries	sprigs of oregano or marjoram

Sterilize your jars and lids (see page 146).

Put the wine, vinegar, sugar, salt, oil, chilli (if using), bay leaf and juniper into a large saucepan. Place over a medium-low heat and bring slowly to the boil.

Peel and cut any carrots and fennel into strips or cubes. Top and tail any green beans, peel any onions and pod any peas or broad beans (fava beans).

When the pickle liquid comes to the boil, increase the heat to medium, add the vegetables and garlic, then return to the boil. Stir in the herbs, then switch off the heat and drain immediately through a sieve placed over a large bowl, reserving the liquid.

Fill the jars with the vegetables and aromatics, topping up with the pickling liquid. Keep in the fridge, or sterilize the filled jars, as below, to keep them for up to 4 months.

Cover the base of your largest saucepan with a clean, folded tea towel, or a trivet. Seal the jars and transfer to the pan. Fill the pan with enough water to come just below the jar lids and place over a low heat. Bring slowly to the boil, then reduce the heat and simmer for 30 minutes. Leave to cool in the water.

Take the jars out, dry, label and store in a cool dark place. Use after 1 month and within 4 months.

Opposite, clockwise from front: La giardiniera primavera *of mixed vegetables, baby fennel and asparagus*

Baby (bell) pepper antipasto with fennel flowers

Many supermarkets have started to sell mixed colour baby (bell) peppers, which cry out to be preserved. If you don't want to use fennel, flavour the pickle with a couple of peeled crushed garlic cloves, or a piece of (or whole) chilli. Try preserving sliced or baby aubergines (eggplants) this way, too.

Makes 500g (1lb 2oz) jar, or equivalent smaller jars

8–12 mixed colour baby (bell) peppers

fine sea salt

75ml (2½fl oz/⅓ cup) rosé or white wine

75ml (2½fl oz/⅓ cup) white wine vinegar

75ml (2½fl oz/⅓ cup) water

2 teaspoons sea salt flakes

2 teaspoons caster (superfine) sugar

3 fennel flower heads, or fennel fronds, or ½ teaspoon fennel seeds

Pierce each (bell) pepper with a fine-pronged fork and layer in a colander with the salt. Cover with a plate, put a weight on top and leave overnight, covered with a clean cloth.

Put the wine, vinegar and water in a saucepan with the salt flakes, sugar and fennel flower heads, fronds or fennel seeds. Place over a medium-low heat and bring gently to a simmer, stirring to dissolve the sugar. Switch off, cover and leave to cool overnight.

In the morning, rinse the (bell) peppers and leave to drain on a clean cloth, or pat them dry. Strain the pickling liquid through a sieve into a large bowl, retaining the fennel.

When the (bell) peppers are quite dry, layer in a sterilized jar (see page 146) with the fennel flower heads, fronds or seeds. Top up the jar with the cooled pickling liquid and seal. Store in the fridge and use after 1 month. This will keep for 6 months or more.

Rice vinegar pickled samphire (salicornia)

Rice vinegar pickles — or *su-zuki* as they are called in Japan — are one of my favourites. Their subtle balance of sweetness and acidity is delicious added to salads, or with any of the oriental fish and meat recipes in the book.

Makes 500g (1lb 2oz) jar, or equivalent smaller jars

200g (7oz) samphire (salicornia)

1 teaspoon fine sea salt (for other less salty veggies, use 2% salt to vegetable weight)

200ml (7fl oz/scant 1 cup) rice vinegar

100ml (3½fl oz/scant ½ cup) mirin

Rinse the samphire (salicornia) in at least 2 changes of water, then drain. Pick over it, discarding tough bits or anything brownish, then scatter over a tea towel to dry. Spread the dry samphire (salicornia) on a large dish, sprinkle with the salt, cover and leave overnight. Rinse well to get rid of the salt, then drain, lay on a clean cloth and pat dry, picking out any bits that look a bit slimy. Pack into a sterilized jar (see page 146).

Mix the vinegar and mirin and add to the jar, seal and store in the dark. Use after 1 week; this will keep for 3 months.

RAW AND RARE

Opposite: Mixed mushroom salad pickle with garlic and coriander (see page 154) This page: Pickled gooseberries with cardamom and star anise (see page 155)

Mixed mushroom salad pickle with garlic and coriander

This recipe was inspired by a mix of exotic mixed mushrooms on sale at my greengrocer. I've used my favourite combination of mushrooms, garlic and coriander seeds to complete the basic pickle. If you enjoy foraging (and – importantly – you know what you are doing!), this is a great way to preserve a glut of field and other wild mushrooms. Serve as part of a sharing platter, in salads, or with seared meat and fish dishes.

Makes 500–750g (1lb 2oz–1lb 10oz) jar, or equivalent smaller jars

300–450g (10½oz–1lb) mixed mushrooms, such as shiitake, enoki, straw and so on

extra virgin olive oil

5 garlic cloves, peeled and crushed with the side of a knife

1 teaspoon fine sea salt

freshly ground black pepper

300ml (10fl oz/1¼ cups) cider vinegar

100ml (3½fl oz/scant ½ cup) water

2 teaspoons sugar

2 teaspoons coriander seeds

Cut any large mushrooms into pieces and divide any mushroom clusters into sections.

Put a heavy-based saucepan over a low heat and, when warm, add enough oil to cover the base. Add the garlic and cook gently until transparent. Discard the garlic.

Add the large mushroom pieces to the saucepan and cook gently for a few minutes, turning to absorb the oil on all sides, then transfer to a plate. Add a little extra oil to the pan and add the pieces of mushroom clusters and any smaller mushrooms; cook for a couple of minutes, turning once, to allow them to absorb the oil. Put these with the other mushrooms, season with the salt and pepper and leave to cool.

Put the vinegar, water, sugar and coriander seeds in a saucepan and bring gently to a simmer. Switch off the heat and leave to cool. Strain over a large bowl once cold, reserving the liquid and the coriander seeds.

When the mushrooms and the pickling fluid are both cold, layer the mushroom pieces and coriander seeds in a sterilized jar (see page 146). Top up the jar with the cooled pickling liquid and seal. Store in a dark cupboard. Use after 1 month, or keep for up to 6 months.

Pickled gooseberries with cardamom and star anise

Gooseberries have a short season, from early- to mid-summer, and are mainly found in greengrocers, farm shops and markets, so seek them out. Their fresh, acidic flavour make them delicious with fatty fish, while the delicate colour and marble-like form create a stunning garnish. Choose only the firmest berries, so they hold their shape once cooked. For the same reason, make sure they only stay in the hot syrup for literally seconds.

Makes 500g (1lb 2oz) jar, or equivalent smaller jars

350g (12oz) large but firm gooseberries, or small firm plums

200ml (7fl oz/scant 1 cup) water

150ml (5fl oz/⅔ cup) white wine vinegar

125g (4½oz/⅔ cup) sugar

1 star anise, broken in half

8 cardamom pods, gently crushed, husks discarded

pinch of sea salt

Rinse the gooseberries, then drain and dry them thoroughly on a clean cloth, or in the sun, or in an airy kitchen. Put the water, vinegar and sugar in a small saucepan and bring to the boil, stirring to avoid the sugar burning on the pan. Reduce the heat to a simmer and add the star anise, cardamom seeds and salt.

Have ready a bowl of iced water. Add the gooseberries to the syrup and turn gently to coat the fruit, then immediately, using a slotted spoon, transfer to a small bowl. Immediately sit the bowl of gooseberries in the bowl of iced water. Leave both gooseberries and syrup to cool.

As soon as both are cold, pack the gooseberries into a sterilized jar or jars (see page 146) and top up with syrup, adding the spices as you do so. Make sure the gooseberries stay below the level of the pickle. Seal and label straight away. These will keep for up to 6 months.

Pickled damsons with garlic, chilli and ginger

Although this is an oriental-inspired pickle, the finished fruit is firm and olive like. The damsons can be served with drinks, marinated with chopped herbs and extra virgin olive oil, or used as a side with oriental dishes.

Makes 500g (1lb 2oz) jar, or equivalent smaller jars

500g (1lb 2oz) firm, just-unripe damsons

10g (¼oz/½ tablespoon) sea salt

225ml (7½fl oz/scant 1 cup) rice vinegar

225ml (7½fl oz/scant 1 cup) mirin

2 garlic cloves

piece of root ginger, sliced

1 dried chilli

Wash the damsons, drain, lay on a cloth and leave to dry in the sun or at room temperature. When dry, layer the damsons, sprinkling lightly with the salt, in a sterilized jar or jars (see page 146). Leave for 3 days, then top the jar up with cold water and leave for another 24 hours.

Drain the damsons, rinse and leave to dry as before. When dry, pack them back into the jar, adding the vinegar, mirin, garlic, ginger and chilli. Seal and use after 1 month, or keep for 6 months.

Fragrant sweet-cured julienne of vegetables with ginger

This sweet pickle works well mixed into fresh salads and stir-fries, or simply served on its own as a side dish. It can be eaten three days after making.
If you would like to experiment with the aromatics, try adding a handful of crushed galangal or a couple of crushed lemon grass sticks, instead of ginger.

Makes 1kg (2¼lb) jar, or equivalent smaller jars

750ml (25fl oz/3 cups) white vinegar

500g (1lb 2oz/2¼ cups) granulated sugar

20g (¾oz/½ tablespoon) coarse sea salt

150g (5½oz) carrots

150g (5½oz) spring onions (scallions)

150g (5½oz) celery hearts, fennel or daikon

egg-sized lump of root ginger or galangal, or 1 stick of lemon grass

Put the vinegar, sugar and salt in a saucepan over a low heat and bring gently to simmering point, stirring now and then to dissolve the sugar. Do not boil. Transfer to a jug and leave to cool.

Cut the carrots, spring onions (scallions) and other vegetables into matchstick strips and fill a sterilized jar or jars (see page 146). Cut the ginger into strips and add this to the jar. Top up with the cooled pickling liquid. Seal and use after 3 days, or keep for 1 month or more.

A 'peck' of pickled chilli peppers

Pickling chillies reduces their fiery quality and transforms them into a perfect accompaniment to grilled (broiled) meats, or a delicious and colourful salad ingredient, either finely chopped, cut into julienne, or left whole.

Makes 500g (1lb 2oz) jar, or equivalent smaller jars

125g (4oz) large red chillies

30g (1¼oz) green bird's eye chillies

1 teaspoon fine sea salt

250ml (8½fl oz/1 cup) distilled spiced white vinegar 6% (barley)

15g (½oz/1 tablespoon) sugar

Cut the large chillies in half lengthways, discard the seeds and stalks and arrange them in a single layer in a shallow dish. Trim the bird's eye chillies as necessary; if they are not freshly picked it may be best to pull off the stalks and calyxes. Lay them between the chilli halves. Sprinkle with the salt, cover with a plate, put a weight on top and leave overnight in the fridge.

Put the spiced vinegar and sugar in a small pan and gently bring to simmering point, stirring now and then to make sure the sugar dissolves without catching on the pan. Leave to cool overnight.

In the morning, pour away any liquor that has leached from the chillies. Rinse them briefly in cold water, drain and leave to dry in a folded clean cloth. When quite dry, pack the large chilli halves upright into a sterilized jar or jars (see page 146), push the bird's eye chillies in between and top up with the vinegar solution. Seal and store in a dark cupboard for 1 week before opening. These will keep for 3 months.

From top: Fragrant sweet-cured julienne of vegetables with ginger, A 'peck' of pickled chilli peppers, Pickled damsons with garlic, chilli and ginger (see page 155)

Spreewald pickled gherkins (dill pickles)

Lübbenau is a charming town an hour's drive south of Berlin, Germany; a tiny place set on a network of tree-lined water courses, popular for punting... and sourcing pickled cucumbers. There are countless pickle manufacturers, hectares of cucumber fields, a pickle bicycle path, museum and market.

Makes 500g (1lb 2oz) jar

500g (1lb 2oz) small pickling cucumbers

10g (¼oz/½ tablespoon) fine sea salt, plus 3 heaped teaspoons

1-2 onions, to taste

500ml (17fl oz/2 cups) white wine vinegar

3 teaspoons sugar

2 bay leaves

4 cloves

2 large or 4 small vine (grape) leaves

½ bunch of dill

Wash the cucumbers, then drain and leave on a clean towel to dry. Put in a bowl with the 10g (¼oz) of salt and cover with cold water, stirring to dissolve the salt. Peel the onion(s), cut into rings, add to the cucumbers and leave for 24 hours. Gently massage the cucumbers from time to time in the brine.

Heat the vinegar gently in a pan with the sugar and the 3 heaped teaspoons of salt. When it starts to simmer, add the bay leaves and cloves, then switch off the heat and leave to cool. Wash the vine (grape) leaves and the dill, drain and leave on a clean towel to dry.

After 24 hours, line the bottom of a sterilized jar (see page 146) with a vine leaf or 2. Rinse and dry the cucumbers and onion(s) and pack into the jar, adding a few sprigs of dill. Pour over the cold pickling liquid and cover with the remaining vine leaves. Leave in a cool dark place for 1 month and eat within 6 months.

Sweet-and-sour Swedish pickled onions

The mixed colour baby onions I used for the photo opposite look pretty, but white onions are just as good a way to enjoy the sweet-and-sour quality of a Swedish pickle. I flavoured them with spices, but the original pickle would be flavoured with dill. Allow 20g (¾oz) of small dill fronds, if using dill.

Makes 500g (1lb 2oz) jar, or equivalent smaller jars

150ml (5fl oz/⅔ cup) white wine vinegar, or cider vinegar

1 teaspoon black peppercorns

1 teaspoon mustard seeds

150g (5½oz/⅔ cup) granulated sugar

1 level teaspoon fine sea salt

500g (1lb 2oz) baby mixed colour or white onions, or mixed onions and shallots

Put 200ml (6¾fl oz/generous ¾ cup) of water, the vinegar, spices, sugar and salt in a saucepan and gently bring to simmering point, stirring now and then to make sure the sugar dissolves without burning. When the pickle starts to simmer, add the onions and, when the liquid returns to the boil, use a slotted spoon to transfer them to a bowl. Leave the onions and the pickle to cool.

Once cold, pack the onions into a sterilized jar or jars (see page 146) and top up with the cooled pickling liquid and spices. Seal and label. Keep for 1 month before opening; these will keep for 6 months.

Fruit

Watermelon cuts with matcha granita

Chlorophyll-coloured matcha tea powder has a fine, distinct bitter flavour and is a pleasant-yet-acquired taste. Fusing Italian granita (water-ice normally flavoured with coffee or citrus) with Japanese matcha tea is my own take. Try it in hot weather to cool yourself down. Served with watermelon, it makes an exceptionally pretty, cooling and wonderfully refreshing dessert. Make the granita well ahead, as it takes hours to freeze, so be patient!

Serves 8

For the granita

200g (7oz/scant 1 cup) granulated sugar

750ml (25fl oz/3 cups) water

10g (¼oz/4 teaspoons) matcha green tea powder

For the watermelon

1 small or ½ large watermelon, chilled

Start with the granita. Put the sugar and water in a saucepan over a medium-low heat and gently bring to simmering point. Stir from time to time to dissolve the sugar.

Leave to cool for 20 minutes, then whisk in the matcha.

When completely cold, put in a covered bowl in the bottom of a freezer. Whisk every 20 minutes until the matcha turns to ice crystals; this will take several hours. (Otherwise, use an ice-cream maker.) Transfer to plastic containers and store until required.

Put 8 serving plates in the freezer 1 hour before serving.

Cut the watermelon into 12 half-circle slices, each 1–2cm (½–¾in) thick. Cut 8 of the half-circles in half again and arrange 2 of these cuts, point to point, towards the centre of each cold serving plate, leaving room for a ball of the granita. Cut the other 4 half-cuts into quarters and arrange 2 of these on top of the bigger slices of watermelon (see photo, right).

Fill an ice-cream scoop with the matcha granita and pack it down well. Turn out into the middle of each chilled serving plate and serve at once.

VARIATION: For lemon granita, use 250ml (8½fl oz/1 cup) lemon juice (about 5 lemons), the finely grated zest of 1 unwaxed lemon, 250ml (8½fl oz/1 cup) water and 250g (9oz/1¼ cups) sugar. For coffee granita, use 500ml (17fl oz/2 cups) strong coffee and 250g (9oz/1¼ cups) sugar.

Yellow nectarines with black cherries and maraschino

The contrast in colours here between ripe, rich yellow nectarines and dark red cherries in the bowl is a feast for the eyes; the flavour of the fruit and liqueur, a party for the taste buds.

Serves 6

4 large, ripe yellow nectarines	2 tablespoons Cointreau or Maraschino liqueur
2 handfuls of plump ripe black cherries	icing (confectioners') sugar, to taste

Halve the nectarines, discard the stones and cut each half into 4 wedges. Put them in a bowl.

Cut the cherries in half and discard the stones. Put the cherry halves in the bowl with the liqueur and stir well. Add icing (confectioners') sugar to taste.

VARIATION: Try this with apricot halves and whole blueberries, with Amaretto liqueur.

White peach and raspberry platter

There are so many fruit combinations that, creatively arranged, make delicious desserts; however, the fruit must be plump and really ripe-but-firm, as both texture and sweetness are all-important. This recipe calls for white peaches, but if, when you go shopping, yellow peaches or white nectarines are riper and firmer, choose those instead.

Serves 4

200g (7oz/1½ cups) raspberries

icing (confectioners') sugar, to taste

4 ripe white peaches

4 bunches of redcurrants, 4 large cherries on stalks, or 4 plump raspberries

Put the raspberries in a mouli-legumes (food mill) and purée; or press them through a sieve. Add sifted icing (confectioners') sugar to taste. Cut each peach into 6 wedges and discard the stones. Do not peel.

Pour the raspberry purée into 4 large dessert dishes and, using the back of a tablespoon, spread it out to cover the plates.

Arrange 3 peach wedges in a line, starting at the rim, stone side facing the middle, and finishing at the centre. Now complete the row across the middle of the plate in a straight line with another 3 slices, facing the opposite way. Take care not to splash the raspberry purée on the peach slices. Garnish with a bunch of redcurrants, a large stemmed cherry or a raspberry.

'Cebiche' pear with lime and chilli

Choose firm, sweet, juicy, slightly under-ripe dessert pears for this dish.
They need to be crisp, so you are able to cut them into thin slices. The
dressing of lime, sugar and chilli creates a lovely fresh, zingy combination
of taste and textures. Note that this must all be made at the last minute,
so do not be tempted to squeeze the citrus or chop the chilli in advance.

Serves 4

1 red chilli

4 crisp/hard dessert pears with stalks

4 pear leaves, or basil or mint leaves

juice of 4 small limes

4 tablespoons caster (superfine) sugar

When ready to serve, cut the chilli in half, discard the seeds and the white ribs, then chop very finely.

Take a pear and cut it horizontally into thin slices; leaving the top 2–3cm (¾–1¼in) of the pear, including the stalk, whole. Fix a pear leaf (or basil or mint leaf) to the stalk part and put to one side.

Spread the slices out in a circle on a large plate, in the order in which they were cut. You are going to have to re-build the pear in a moment so keep the slices in order.

Squeeze the lime juice over the slices and then sprinkle over the sugar. Top with a little of the chilli to taste and then stack up the slices to re-build the pear.

Complete the pear by adding the stalk part, decorated with the leaf. Set in the centre of a serving plate. Spoon any remaining juices over and around the pear.

Working quickly, repeat to assemble the other pears.

Pineapple carpaccio with orange and passion fruit

It is hard to believe that, when the humdrum pineapple debuted on our shores, it caused such excitement and was so highly prized that its aristocratic growers had to provide an armed guard when the fruit travelled between country estate and town house.

If you have a meat slicer, cut the pineapple paper-thin with that, or cut it as thinly as possible using a sharp knife.

Serves 6

1 pineapple	icing (confectioners') sugar, to taste	4 passion fruits
4 tablespoons Amaretto or Cointreau liqueur	4 small oranges	

Prepare the pineapple. Cut off the leaves, then peel, and finally dig out the eyes. Slice very thinly and arrange on a platter. Chop any off-cuts into bits and use them to fill the centre of a serving dish. Splash with liqueur and dust generously with icing (confectioners') sugar.

Cut the orange peel away from the fruit, removing the white pith at the same time. Cut the oranges into slices and arrange these in a ring on the pineapple slices.

Cut the passion fruits in half lengthways, scoop the flesh out and spread a thin veil of it over the oranges and the chopped pineapple in the centre of the dish.

VARIATIONS: Serve with pomegranate jewels, or serve sliced oranges and tangerines this way with blueberries and Grand Marnier.

Persimmon shell with mint and sake-mandarin dressing

The simplest way to serve a persimmon — the flesh being so sweet and rich — is as nature intended. Alternatively, cut off the lid, stick it back on top, freeze for a few hours and serve from the freezer with a grapefruit spoon to dig out the flesh. However, that seems a bit like a cop-out in a recipe book, so here is my riff on that classic.

For a sensuous drink, whizz the frozen mix below until smooth and serve in cocktail glasses with the persimmon 'hat' cocked on the side.

Serves 4

4 large, ripe persimmons	1 tablespoon sake
juice of 2 large mandarins	12 mint leaves, finely chopped

Cut the top off the persimmons and reserve. Scoop out the flesh, leaving a shell 5mm (¼in) thick.

Chop the flesh evenly by hand; don't use a food processor or it will become liquid. Put it in a bowl and add the mandarin juice, sake and mint. Mix and return to the persimmon shells, putting the hats back on.

Store in the fridge and then freeze for 90 minutes or so, before serving straight from the freezer.

Grilled (broiled) fig flowers with marsala and orange

The fig is one of my favourite fruits, and best enjoyed straight from the tree. In their native Mediterranean countries, they are so prolific that big old trees, heavy with fruit, are often left abandoned. Come late summer, friendly fig fights rage between warring teenagers.

Serves 4

4 large figs

2 small bananas

1 tablespoon lime juice

juice of 1 orange

4 tablespoons Marsala

flaked (slivered) almonds

2–4 teaspoons demerara (raw brown) sugar

Preheat a grill (broiler) to medium-high.

Split the figs open with a cross cut, starting from the stalk end, but do not cut them through the base. Open each fruit up like the petals of a flower. Arrange the cut figs in an ovenproof dish or baking tray.

Mash the bananas in a dish to a smooth paste, mix with the lime juice and spoon into each fig.

Pour the orange juice and Marsala over the figs, top each with a few flaked (slivered) almonds and sprinkle with sugar.

Grill (broil) for 10 minutes – watch carefully, as the almonds catch quickly – then serve at once.

Index

About the author

Food writer, cook, teacher and traveller Lindy Wildsmith is a great believer in the importance of seasonal ingredients and connecting with the land, people and producers she meets. Her book *Cured* was shortlisted for the André Simon award and the Guild of Food Writers best food book. Her most recent book, *Artisan Drinks*, celebrated the pleasure to be had from making your own everything, from tisanes to champagne. She also wrote *Cichetti: and Other Small Italian Dishes to Share*, with Valentina Harris.

Lindy worked with Chef Franco Taruschio OBE (founder of the famed Walnut Tree Inn) for 15 years at the Chef's Room, the award-winning cookery school in Wales. Lindy now organizes pop-up corporate and bespoke private cooking events. Lindy teaches preserving and curing at The School of Artisan Food at Welbeck in Nottinghamshire, and Italian cooking at the WI cookery school, Denman College, near Abingdon. You can follow her on twitter @lindywildsmith and on Facebook.

My thanks to:

The creative team: Kevin Summers, Maggie Town and Cynthia Inions; and the editorial team at Jacqui Small.

Yoshinori Ishii, executive chef at Umu, Mayfair, London, appointed as Japanese cuisine goodwill ambassador by the Japanese government.

Takashi Mizutani and Chikako Yamamoto, Kochi Prefecture Government Trade Association. Sei Hamaguchi (toyokunijapan.com).

Daniele Codini and Yashin Ocean House, South Kensington.

The Japanese Embassy and Jetro in London.

Martin Morales, restaurateur, chef, author and unofficial Peruvian ambassador of food and culture in London.

Franco Taruschio.

Amanda Stradling, Veggies Galore, Ross-on-Wye, Herefordshire.

Annegret Schrick, consultant, Essen, Germany.